A-Z ASHFORD, FOLKESTONE a

CON

Key to Map Pages	2-
Large Scale Town Centres	4-
Map Pages	8-6

65-84

REFERENCE

Motorway	**M20**
A Road	**A20**
B Road	**B2011**
Dual Carriageway	
One-way Street Traffic flow on A roads is also indicated by a heavy line on the driver's left.	
Road Under Construction Opening dates are correct at the time of publication.	
Proposed Road	
Restricted Access	
Pedestrianized Road	
Track	
Footpath	
Residential Walkway	
Railway	Station / Heritage Station / Level Crossing / Tunnel
Built-up Area	
Local Authority Boundary	
Posttown Boundary	
Postcode Boundary (within posttown)	
Map Continuation	8 / Large Scale Town Centre 4

Car Park (selected)	P
Church or Chapel	†
Cycleway (selected)	⬤⬤⬤
Fire Station	■
Hospital	Ⓗ
House Numbers (A & B Roads only)	10 ... 124
Information Centre	ℹ
National Grid Reference	630
Police Station	▲
Post Office	★
Safety Camera with Speed Limit Fixed cameras and long term road works cameras. Symbols do not indicate camera direction.	(30)
Toilet: without facilities for the Disabled with facilities for the Disabled Disabled use only	▽ ▽ ▽
Educational Establishment	▢
Hospital or Healthcare Building	▢
Industrial Building	▢
Leisure or Recreational Facility	▢
Place of Interest	▢
Public Building	▢
Shopping Centre or Market	▢
Other Selected Buildings	▢

SCALE

Map Pages 8-64	Large Scale Pages 4, 5, 6-7
1:15,840 4 inches (10.16) to 1 mile, 6.31cm to 1 km	1:7,920 8 inches (20.32cm) to 1 mile 12.63cm to 1km

0 ¼ ½ Mile
0 250 500 750 Metres

0 ⅛ ¼ Mile
0 100 200 300 Metres

Copyright of Geographers' A-Z Map Company Limited

Fairfield Road, Borough Green, Sevenoaks, Kent TN15 8PP
Telephone: 01732 781000 (Enquiries & Trade Sales)
01732 783422 (Retail Sales)

www.az.co.uk

Copyright © Geographers' A-Z Map Co. Ltd.

Edition 5 2012

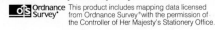

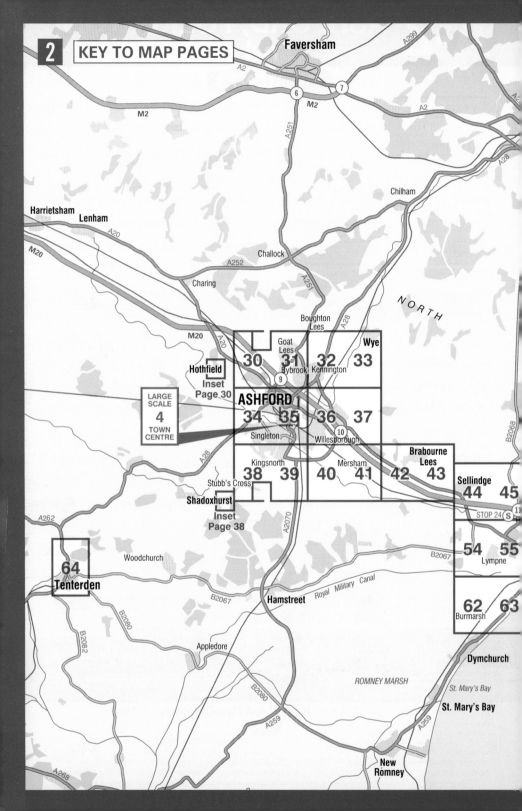

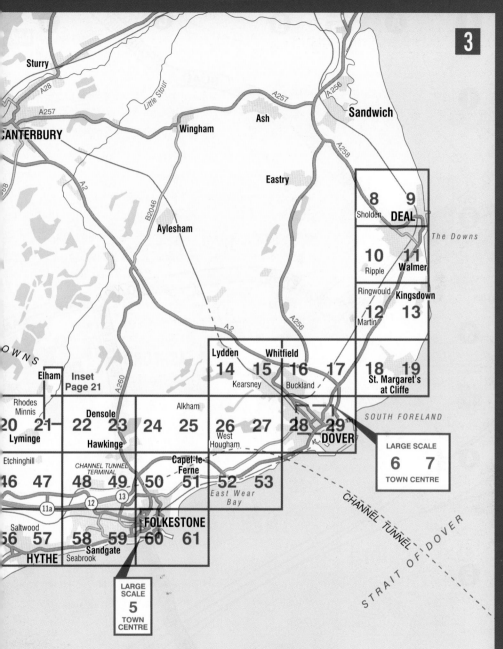

3

Sturry

A28

CANTERBURY

A257

A2

Little Stour

Wingham

Ash

A257

A256

Sandwich

A258

Eastry

DEAL

8   9

Sholden

The Downs

10   11

Ripple   Walmer

Ringwould   Kingsdown

12   13

Martin

Aylesham

B2046

A2

A256

Lydden   Whitfield

14   15   16   17   18   19

Kearsney   Buckland   St. Margaret's at Cliffe

Elham

Inset Page 21

Rhodes Minnis   Densole   Alkham

20   21   22   23   24   25   26   27   28   29

Lyminge   Hawkinge   West Hougham   DOVER

SOUTH FORELAND

LARGE SCALE
6   7
TOWN CENTRE

Etchinghill   CHANNEL TUNNEL TERMINAL   Capel-le-Ferne

46   47   48   49   50   51   52   53

11a   12   13   *East Wear Bay*

Saltwood   FOLKESTONE

56   57   58   59   60   61

HYTHE   Sandgate   Seabrook

LARGE SCALE
5
TOWN CENTRE

CHANNEL TUNNEL

STRAIT OF DOVER

ENGLISH   CHANNEL

SCALE

0   1   2 Miles

0   1   2   3 Kilometres

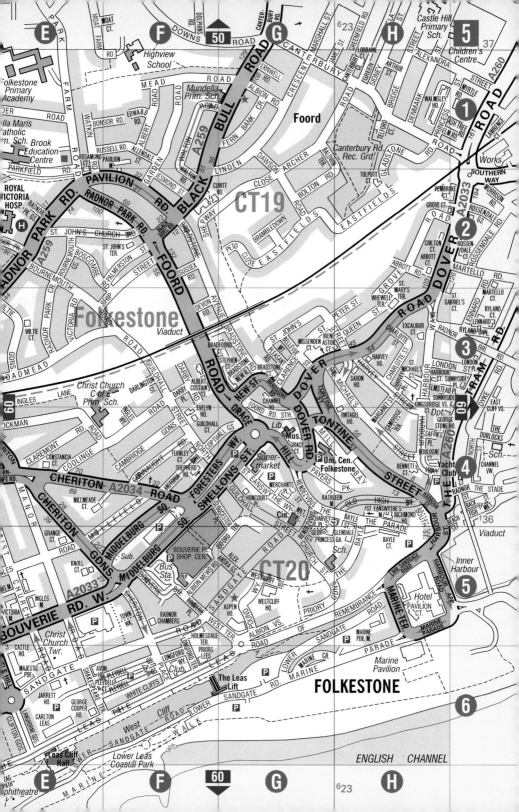

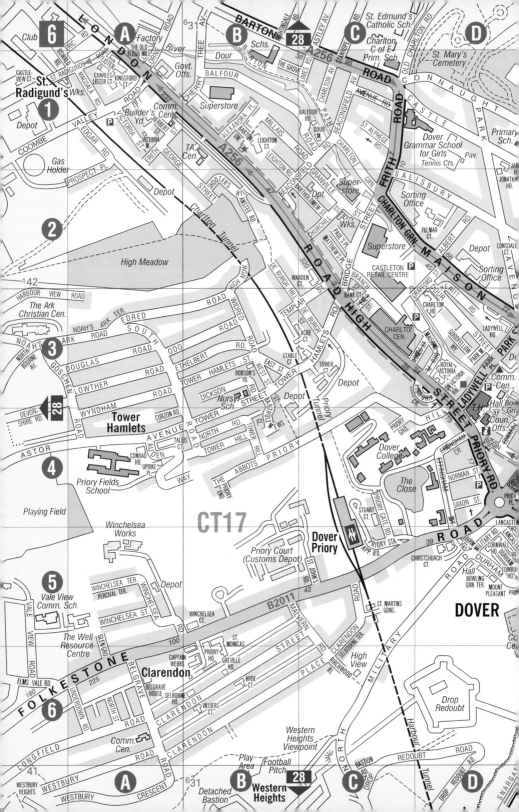

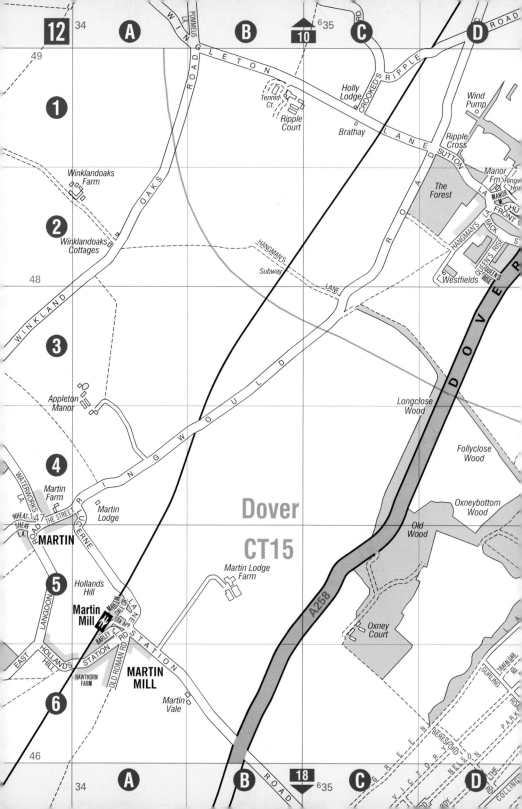

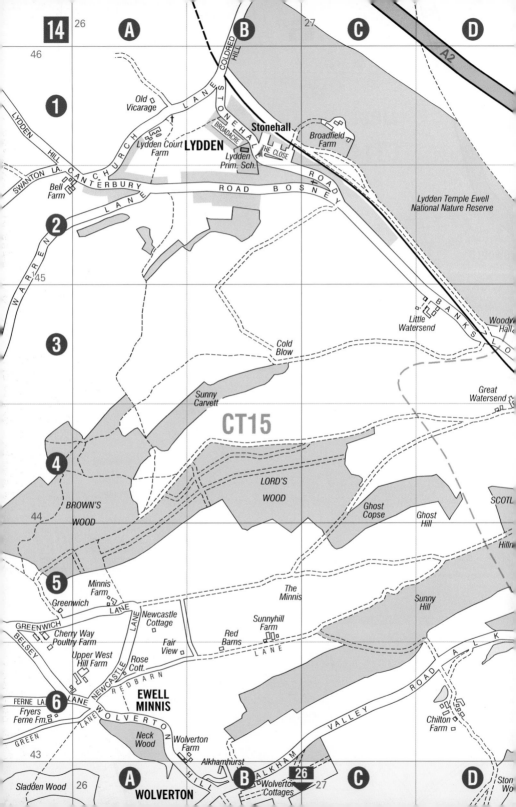

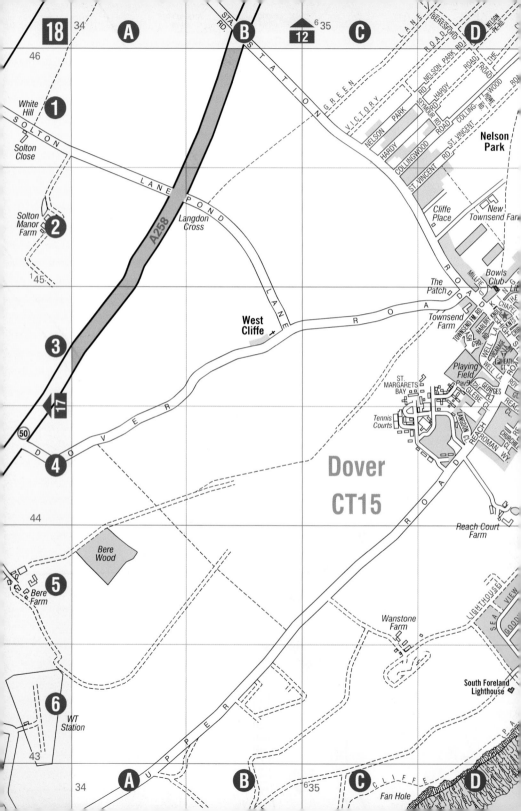

Free Down

Barrow Mount

THE LEAS

Ridgeview

St. Margaret's
Free Down

Feathers

Hog's
Bush

Bockell

The Cut

Free
Down

Signal
Station

Dover Patrol
Memorial

Bockell
Hill

Alexander
Playing
Field

THE RISE

NORMAN RD

VICTORIA AV.

DROVEWAY

The Leas

Coney Burrow
Point

DROVEWAY

CONVENT
CL.

KENILWORTH CL.

St. Margaret's
at Cliffe Sch. &
Portal Ho. Schs.

SALISBURY

GRANVILLE

HOTEL HILL

BAY HILL

BAY

ST. MARGARET'S
BAY

STREET

DOWNSIDE

Bay
Hill

BAY ROAD

Long
Steps

St. Margaret's
Museum

Ness Point

THE

. MARGARET'S
AT CLIFFE

COPELAND RD.

Pines
Gdn.

Ten.
Cts.

LIGHTHOUSE

ST. MARGARET'S RD.

MARGARET'S

FORELAND ROAD

CRESCENT

THE BEACH

ROAD

FRONT

BAY

ROAD

South Foreland
Valley

VIEW
ROAD

GOODWIN RD.

Lighthouse Down

S T R A I T

O F

D O V E R

St. Margaret's Bay
Smockmill
(Closed)

Old
Lighthouse

The
Parlour

S T R A I T

O F

D O V E R

SOUTH FORELAND

1

2

45

3

4

44

5

6

43

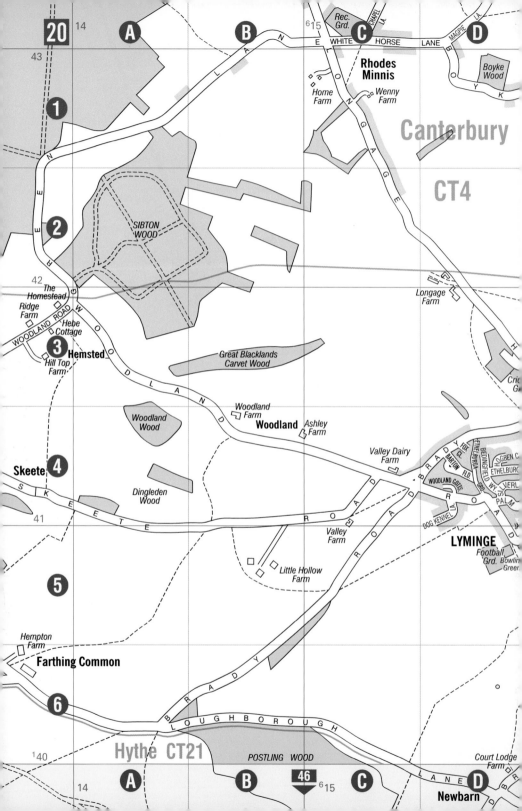

A

B

C

D

Rec. Grd.

CHAPEL LA.

WHITE HORSE LANE

MAGPIE LA.

Rhodes Minnis

Boyke Wood

Home Farm

Wenny Farm

1

Canterbury

CT4

2

SIBTON WOOD

42

Longage Farm

The Homestead

Ridge Farm

WOODLAND ROAD

Hebe Cottage

3 **Hemsted**

Hill Top Farm

Great Blacklands Carvet Wood

Cric Gr

Woodland Farm

Woodland Wood

Woodland

Ashley Farm

Valley Dairy Farm

BRADY RD

FOX CL.

ETHELBURGA

BEDINGFIELD

SGBEN C

ETHELBURC

BARTON

WOODLAND COTS.

VERL

PAL

Skeete **4**

SKEETE

Dingleden Wood

WOODLAND ROAD

DOG KENNEL LA.

RD.

LYMINGE

41

Valley Farm

Football Grd.

Bowlin Greer

5

Little Hollow Farm

Hempton Farm

Farthing Common

BRADY

6

BRADY

LOUGHBOROUGH

LANE

Court Lodge Farm

140

Hythe CT21

POSTLING WOOD

46 615

Newbarn

14

A

B

C

D

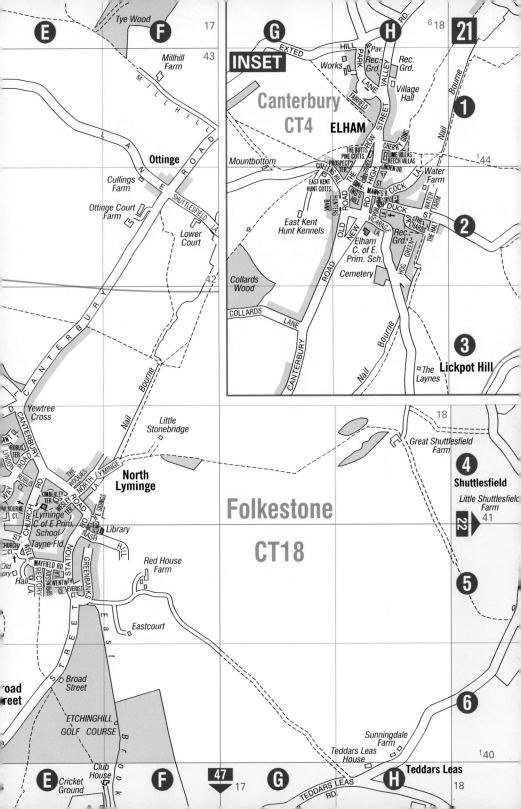

INSET

Canterbury
CT4

ELHAM

EXTED
HILL
PARK LANE
VALLEY
Bourne
Nail

Works
Pav.
Rec.
Grd.
Rec.
Grd.

FAIRFIELD

Village
Hall

Millhill
Farm   43

MILLHILL LANE ROAD

Ottinge

Mountbottom

CHERRY GDNS.
THE BUTTS
PINE COTTS.
LIME VILLAS
BEECH VILLAS
PROSPECT TER.
CULLING HILL
LINDEN DR.
Water
Farm   44

EAST KENT
HUNT COTTS.
BANK
THE
KING'S MARK
HIGH ST.
R. COCK
DUCK
WATER LA.

Cullings
Farm

Ottinge Court
Farm

Lower
Court

HUNTERS HILL

East Kent
Hunt Kennels

ORCHARDS
THE HALT
ORCHARDS

Elham
C. of E.
Prim. Sch.

VICARAGE
NEW
HOG GREEN

Rec.
Grd.

SHUTTLESFIELD LANE

Collards
Wood

Cemetery

COLLARDS   LANE

CANTERBURY   ROAD

OLD   ROAD
POUND

CANTERBURY   ROAD

Bourne
Nail

The
Laynes

Lickpot Hill

Yewtree
Cross

Little
Stonebridge

**North
Lyminge**

Great Shuttlesfield
Farm   18

Folkestone

CT18

Shuttlesfield

Little Shuttlesfield
Farm   41

THE WOODES
NORTH LYMINGE
ROAD
ROBUS TER.
KIMBERLEY TER.
WESLEY TER.
SQUINS.

CHURCH RD.
ROBUS CL.
LINDEN TER.
WAY
MILBOURNE CT.
CHURCH CT.

Lyminge
C of E Prim.
School

Library

Tayne Fld.
NASH

Red House
Farm

MAYFIELD RD.
RECTORY
LA.
JOUSINBAS
WENTWTH
CL.
EVERIST CT.
GREENBANKS

Old
Priory

Hall

STATION HILL

Eastcourt

Broad
Street

East   STREET

Brook

road
reet

ETCHINGHILL
GOLF COURSE

Sunningdale
Farm

Teddars Leas
House

Teddars Leas

E   Cricket
Ground   F

47   17

G   TEDDARS LEAS   RD.   H   18

40

Map page: Dover CT15 / Densole / Hawkinge area.

Grid references: E, F, G, H (top and bottom), 1, 2, 3, 4, 5, 6 (right side)

Labels and features:

Ladwood Shaw, The Homestead, Cold Blows, Hoad Farm, Frogshall Cotts., MacFarlane's World of Butterflies, Clevelands

Pinecote, Belmont, Chipdene, Minnis House, Meadow View, FOX, HOLT ROAD, Foxholt Cottage, Little Foxholt

Longcraft Wood, Thorndean, Minnis Beech

Dover CT15

Ridge Hill Plantation, Acorn Cottage, The Mead Cottage, A260, Rosendale, Caroline Cottage, Red House Farm, Pound Farm

Ridge Farm, Ridge Row, A260, Little Densole Farm, THE DENSOLE PADDOCKS

Whitegate Plantation, Mayfield Farm, Black Horse Farm Caravan Club Site, DENSOLE LA., DENSOLE WAY

COACH ROAD, SCHOOL ROAD, Whilhll vett, White Gates, CANTERBURY, STREET, DENSOLE

Quetta, Bush Farm, Woodside, Limes Farm Equestrian Cen., ST. JOHN'S WY, ST. JOHN'S CL., MINTER CL., NURSERY LA., AVENUE, NURSERY CL., CANTERBURY, 377, REINDEN WOOD

Roods Meadow Farm, PAY STREET, PAY, Reinden Wood House

24

Cobham's Rough, Whitepost Wood, Pay Street Farm, Lavender, Sweet Briar, The Cabin, Milgate Farm, STREET, Fernfield Farm, Play Fld., Cricket Ground, Pav., FERNFIELD

illars Wood, CANTERBURY ROAD, SPITFIRE WAY, A260, CANTERBURY ROAD, WAY, COLL, TYE, WOODLAND, 30, BARN HURST LA., MAYPOLE GROVE, MAPP, MILL, KETTLE, CLOUSTON, PERROT, GRAY, HAGGER, DANIELS, MAPLED, FERN, PKKEYS, THE, COWGATE, FERNFIELD LA.

dsole arm, Hawking Cemetery & Crematorium, MUDIE CL., COX, CAMPBEL, STORY, CA BARN, DR., STABLE Cott., MITCHELL, WINTER, WEBSTER, THE BERRIES, MEADOW CL., PASTURE, MAIN, HAWKINGE

Sewage & Works, CEMETERY COTTAGES, GILLMAN, 49, AERODROME RD., AERODROME RD., HEIM, GREBE, DENYS RD., Prim. Sch., BROMLEY, WOSTER, MILL, MAYPLEFIE

E, F, 49, G, H

21, 22, 43, 42, 41, 40, 22

23

43

A **B** 23 **C** **D**

1

Frogshall Cottages den se

Foxholt Cottage

Little Foxholt

Boyington Court

Boyington Wood

Hall Wood

Hop Garden Carvett

Beard's Hall Farm

Pheasantry

Maison Dieu Wood

Ellinge Cottage

Ellinge House

Pea Woo

2

42

und rm

Everden Cottage

Everden

Great Everden Farm

LOCKERINGE

3

23

REINDEN WOOD

en Wood ouse 41

Lockeringe Wood

Broomfield Cottage

Malabar

Fernfield Bungalow

Stombers Stud

Drellingore

LA

4

Fernfield Farm

Play Fld

Cri GR

SKATERS CL

STREET

MILLFIELD

UNDERWOOD

FERNFIELD LANE

Stombers Farm

St. Radigunds House

Sewage Works

STOMBERS

Shadows Hill Wood

Folkestone CT18

5

MAYPOLE GROVE

THE LANE

MAYPO

RED DRIVE

FORD

CLONSTON

KETTLE

GRAY

HAGGER DR.

DANIEL PL.

THE KEYS

FERNFIELD CL.

COWGATE

MAPLEFIELD GDNS.

Avalon

Limuru

DOVER SHEPWAY

Upper Standen Farm

Standen Cottages

6

W.

DR.

WINTER

MITCHELL

BLAND DR.

Ellington

Cowgate Farm

STANDEN LANE

Lower Standen Farm

HAWKINGE

40

CROMA'T

RECTOR

BERRIES

MEADOW CL.

PASTURE

Rose Cottage Firs Farm

Old Hawkinge

50 23

Hawkinge Hall

LA

HO

A 22 **B** **C** **D**

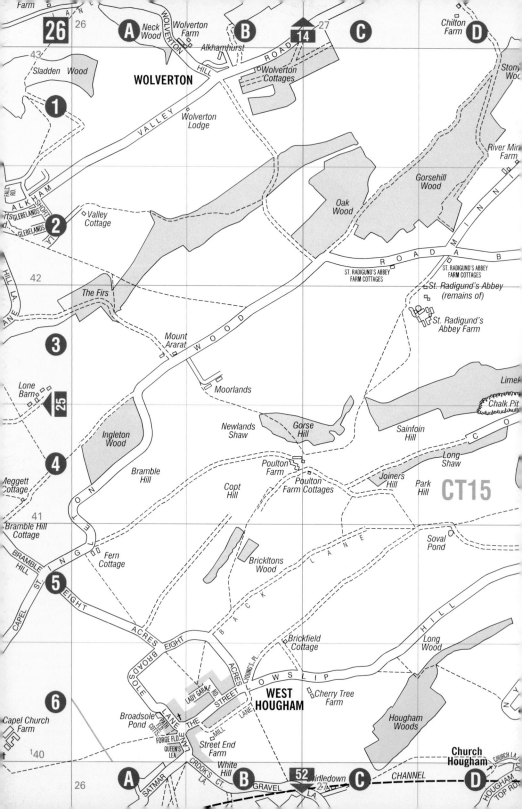

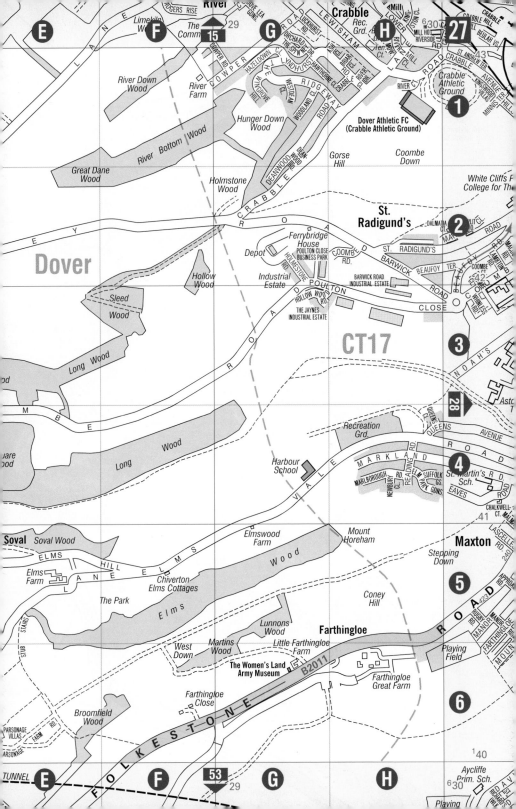

E — **F** — **G** — **H** — **27**

Limekiln Wd

The Comm — 29 — **15**

River

Crabble

Mill

Rec. Grd.

H

6 30 — **43**

27

CRABBLE HILL
BEULAH VS.

CRABBLE

St. ANDREW TER

CRABBLE

River Down Wood

River Farm

Hunger Down Wood

Crabble Athletic Ground

1

Dover Athletic FC
(Crabble Athletic Ground)

Great Dane Wood

River Bottom Wood

Holmstone Wood

Gorse Hill

Coombe Down

White Cliffs
College for Th

Dover

Ferrybridge House

Depot

POULTON CLOSE
BUSINESS PARK

St. Radigund's

DALMATIA CT

2

ROAD

Hollow Wood

Industrial Estate

HOLLOW WOOD

ST. RADIGUND'S

BARWICK

BEAUFOY TER.

COOMBE

Sleed Wood

THE JAYNES
INDUSTRIAL ESTATE

POULTON

BARWICK ROAD
INDUSTRIAL ESTATE

COOMB'
RD.

ROAD

CLOSE

CT17

3

Long Wood

NOAHS

Long Wood

MBE

Recreation Grd.

28

Astc

Harbour School

QUEENS

AVENUE

MARKLAND

ROAD

4

MARLBOROUGH

NEWBURY CL.

READING RD.

SUFFOLK GS.

PARK GDNS.

St. Martin's Sch.

EAVES

CHALKWELL-CT.

Soval — Soval Wood

Elmswood Farm

Mount Horeham

Maxton

LASCELLE

ELMS

HILL

ELMS

Stepping Down

5

Elms Farm

Chiverton Elms Cottages

Wood

APPROA

RUGB

MANOR

FARTHINGLOE

The Park

Elms

Coney Hill

MOUN

STUB STAIRS

Lunnons Wood

Farthingloe

West Down

Martins Wood

Little Farthingloe Farm

The Women's Land Army Museum

B2011

Playing Field

Farthingloe Great Farm

6

PARSONAGE VILLAS

FARM RD.

ARSONAGE

Broomfield Wood

Farthingloe Close

FOLKESTONE

40

E — **F** — **53** — **G** — **H**

TUNNEL

FOLKESTONE

29

Aycliffe Prim. Sch.

6 30

Playing

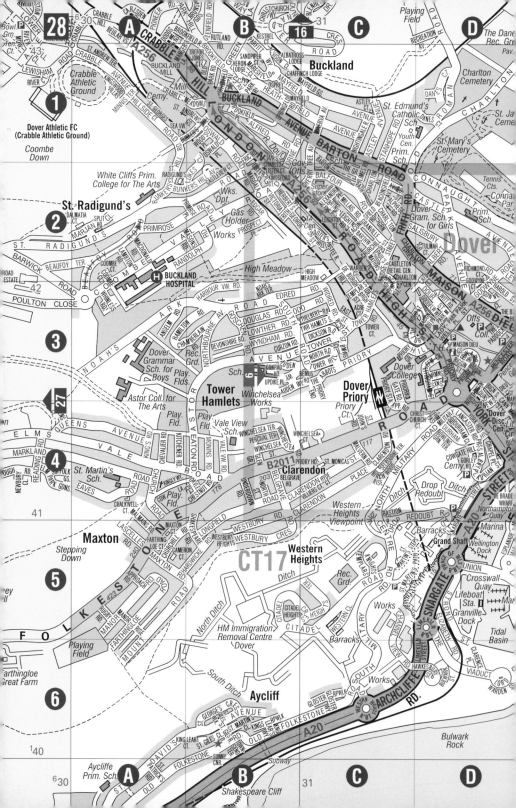

CT15

CT16

TANGIER SQ
CORUNNA CL
DUNKIRK SQ LUCKNOW CL
HEIGHTS KOWLAN KSHA
Comm. ALAMEIN PL.
Cen. TAN PL.
BURGO
ANZIO CRES

Rec. Grd.

Fort Burgoyne
(Casemated Barracks)

Connaught Barracks

Swingate

Edinburgh Hill

Bleriot Memorial

EAST
NORMAN RD.
W NORMAN RD.
GODWIN
HAROLDS
The Keep
Secret Wartime Tunnels
Dover Castle
KNIGHTS
The Pharos
St. Mary in Castro Church
MORTIMER RD.
CANONS GATE
QUEEN ELIZABETH
Moat's Bulwark
Dover Leis. Cen.
ATHOL CLOSE
EAST MARINE

Memorials

①

Coast Guard Station

Langdon Hole

Fox Hill Down

GATEWAY TO THE WHITE CLIFFS
Vis. Cen. **P**

Langdon Cliffs

②

Langdon Cliffs Viewpoint

Depots
COASTGUARD COTTS.
CIRCULAR CAMBER W.
NORTH
CIRCULAR C. CAMBER WY.
Works
EASTERN SERVICE RD.

③

Car Ferry Terminal
INWARD CAR LANES
EAST RAMP
INWARD FREIGHT LANES
NORTH RETURN
WEST RAMP
INWARD CAR LANES
STH. EXIT RD.
LOWER RD.
N. EXT RD.
CENTRAL RD.
UPPER RD.
Works
STH. EXIT RD.
RAMP C
RAMP B
PERIMETER RD.
RAMP A
ENTRANCE R.

STREET MARINE PDE.
A20
Marine Pde Gdns.
THE GATEWAY
MARINE CRES

Eastern Arm

④

DOVER

North Arm

EASTERN DOCKS

42

41

Dover to:
Calais 1 hr. 30 mins
Dunkirk 2 hrs.

O U T E R

H A R B O U R

WESTERN DOCKS

Prince of Wales Pier

North Pier

South Pier

INNER

HARBOUR

Lighthouse

CRUISE LINER TERMINAL

Lighthouse

Southern Breakwater

Lighthouse

Lighthouse

⑤

⑥

STRAIT OF DOVER

Admiralty Pier

40

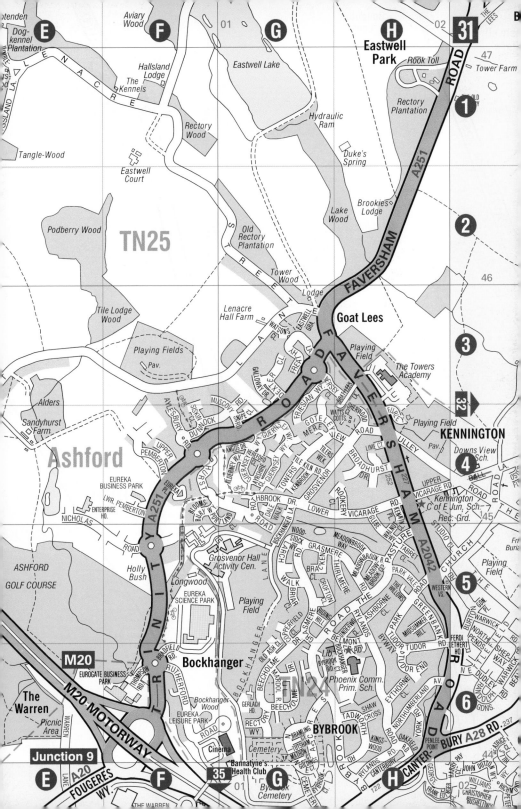

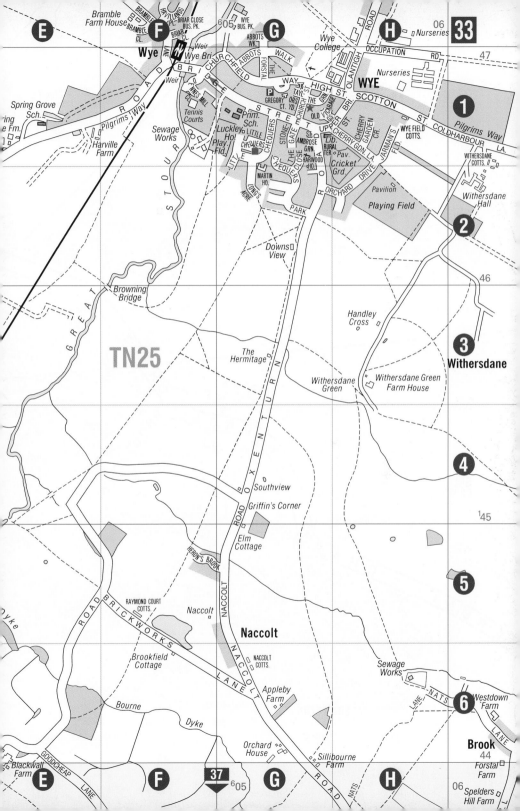

Bramble Farm House
BRAMBLE CL.
BRIAR CLOSE
BUS. PK.
WYE BUS. PK.
605
Wye
ABBOTS WK.
Wye College
OCCUPATION RD.
Nurseries
WYE

Spring Grove Sch.
-ring e Fm.

Pilgrims Way
Harville Farm

Weir
Wye Bri
Wye Bri
Weir
CHURCHFIELD
ABBOTS FORSTAL
THE WALK
HIGH ST.
SCOTTON ST.
OLANTIGH RD.
WYE FIELD COTTS.
Pilgrims Way
COLDHARBOUR LA.

Sewage Works
Tennis Courts
Prim. Sch.
Luckley Ho!
Play. Fld.
LITTLE CHEQUERS
GREGORY CT.
TAYL.
ORS
CH
OLD
THE GRN
UPP. BRI.
CHERRY GDN. LA.
CHERRY GARDEN CR.
JARMAN'S FLD.
WITHERSDANE COTTS.

STONE STREET
THE GATE
AMBROSE GRN.
HARWOOD
Lib.
RURAL
Pav.
Cricket Grd.
Withersdane Hall

MARTIN HO.
CHEQUERS CLOSE
KING'S ACRE
ORCHARD
Pavilion
Playing Field

LITTLE CHEQUERS
PARK

Sewage Works
Downs View
Browning Bridge

GREAT STOUR

TN25

The Hermitage
OXEN TURN ROAD

Handley Cross

Withersdane Green
Withersdane Green Farm House
Withersdane

Southview
Griffin's Corner
Elm Cottage

HERON'S BROOK
NACCOLT LANE

Raymond Court Cotts.
Naccolt
Naccolt

BRICKWORKS LANE
ROAD

Brookfield Cottage
Naccolt
NACCOLT COTTS.

Bourne
Dyke

Appleby Farm

Sewage Works
NATS LANE
Westdown Farm
Brook

Blackwall Farm
GOODCHEAP LANE

Orchard House
Sillibourne Farm
ROAD

Forstal Farm
Spelders Hill Farm

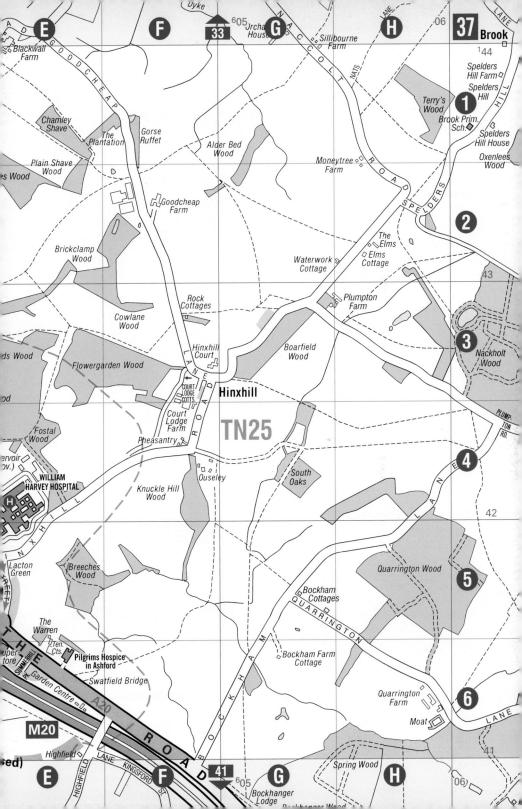

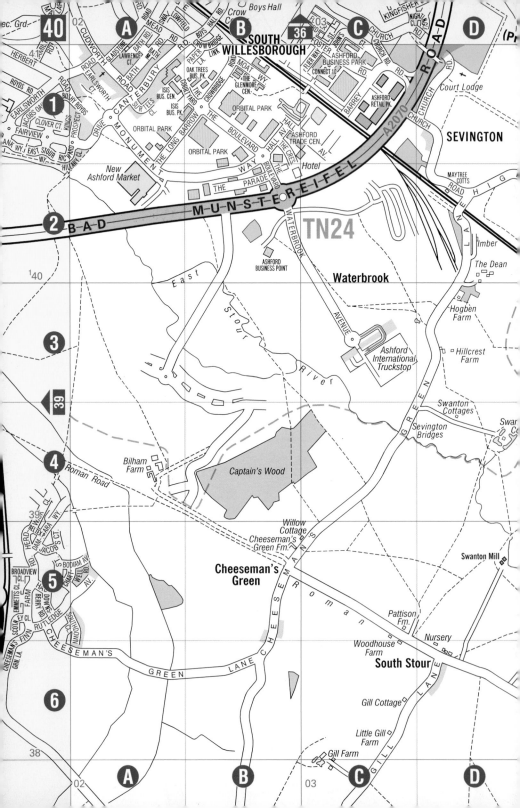

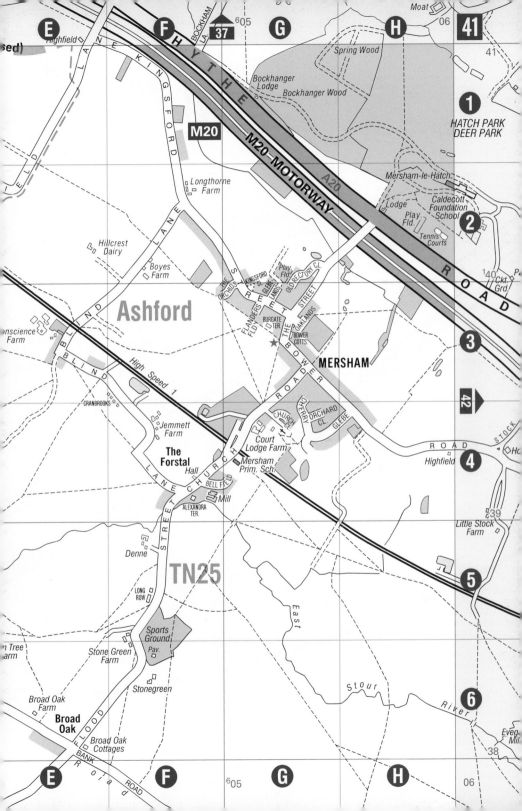

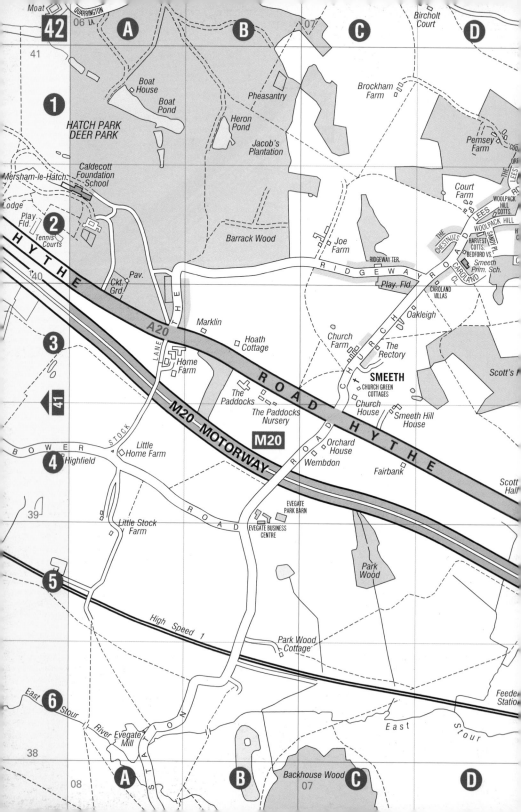

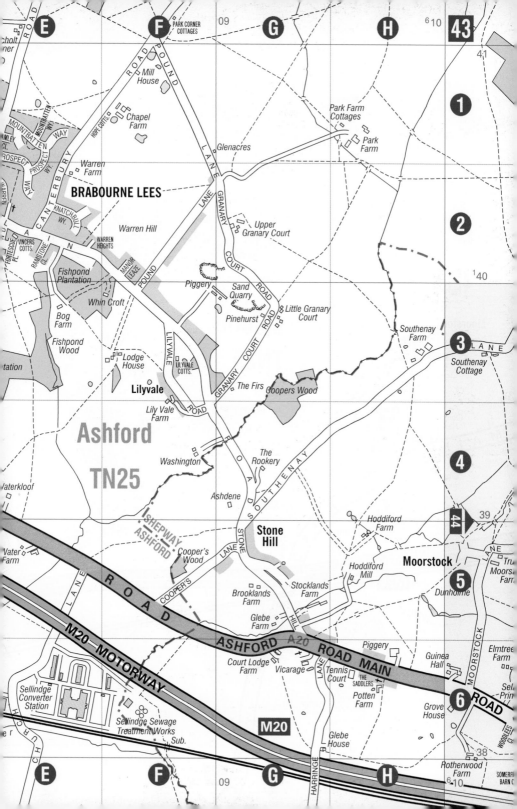

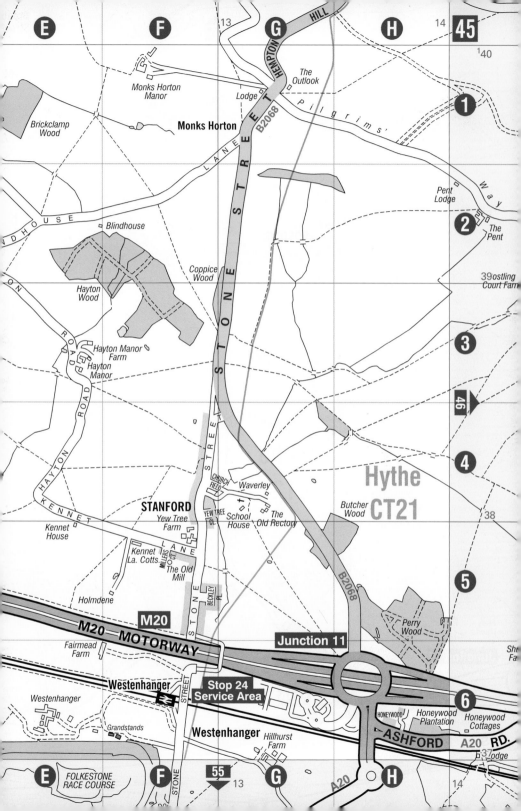

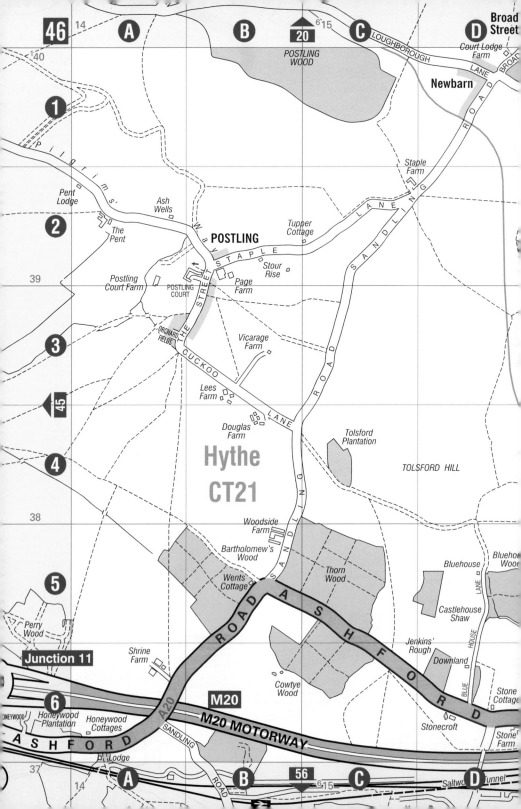

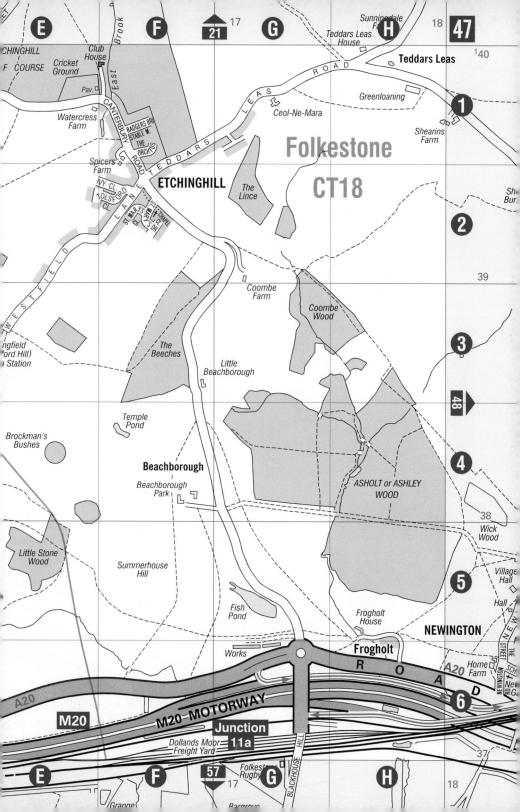

Folkestone

CT18

CHINGHILL
F COURSE

Club House

Cricket Ground

Pav.

Watercress Farm

Spicers Farm

IVY CL
OLSFORD CL.

ST MARY'S CL
HWN ST
CHAPEL DR.

BADGERS BRI
STABLE M.
THE ORCHIS

ETCHINGHILL

The Lince

East Brook

CANTERBURY ROAD

TEDDARS

LANE

WESTFIELD

LEAS ROAD

Teddars Leas

Teddars Leas House

Greenloaning

Ceol-Ne-Mara

Shearins Farm

Sh
Bur

1

2

'40

39

Coombe Farm

Coombe Wood

ngfield
ford Hill)
a Station

The Beeches

Little Beachborough

3

48

4

Temple Pond

Brockman's Bushes

Beachborough

Beachborough Park

ASHOLT or ASHLEY WOOD

38

Wick Wood

Little Stone Wood

Summerhouse Hill

Fish Pond

Froholt House

5

Village Hall

Hall

NEWINGTON

NEWINGTON STREET
THE
SCH
New RD.

Works

Froholt

A20

ROAD

Home Farm

A20

6

D

A20

M20

M20 MOTORWAY

Dollands Moor
Freight Yard

**Junction
11a**

BLACKHOUSE HILL

37

Grange

Bargrove

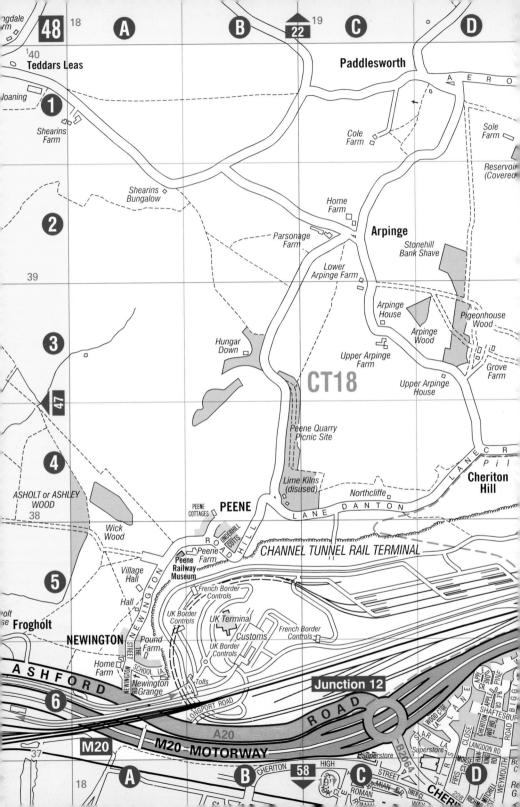

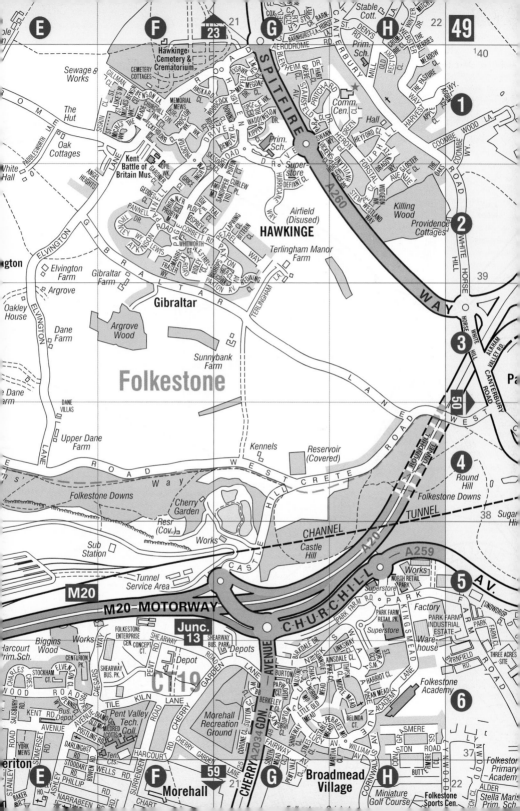

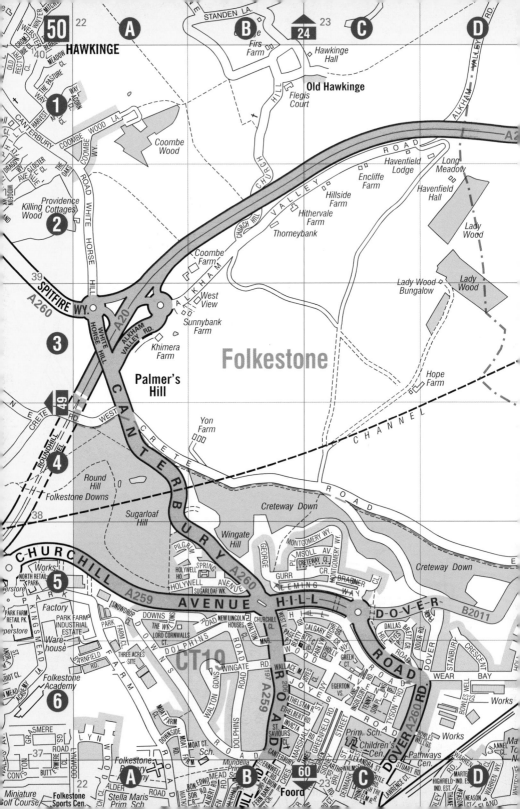

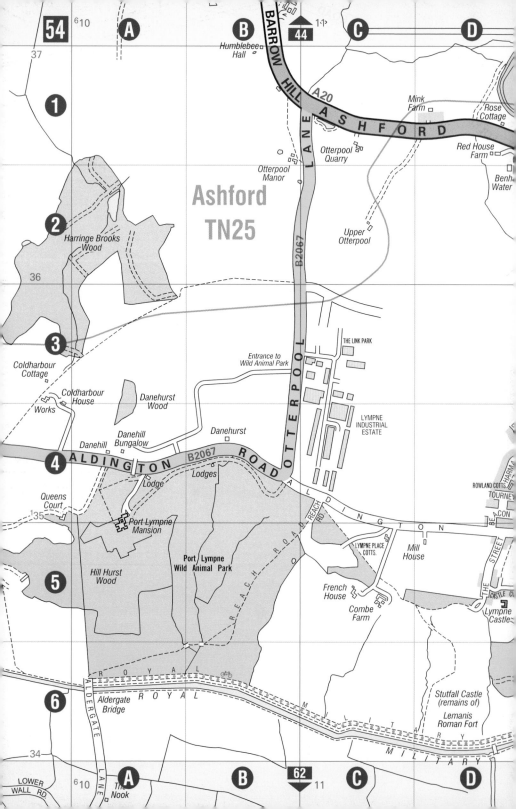

55
45
13
63
E
F
G
H
1
2
3
4
5
6
56
Grandstands
Honeywood Plantation
Honeywood Cottages
14
Lodge
37
ASHFORD ROAD
Hillhurst Farm
FOLKESTONE RACECOURSE
MEADOW CT.
STONE STREET
Westenhanger
Sandling Park
House Wood
Twin Chimneys
A20
Little Greys
Killymoon
Depot
ASHFORD ROAD
The Willows
Elms Farm
KILN WOOD
ROAD
HYTHE
Newingreen
Newingreen Farm
STREET
Black Hill
36
Ashford Lodge
A261
Ivy Cottage
Berwick House
Pedlinge
Pedlinge Farm
FOLKS' WOOD
FOLKS WOOD WY.
FARM CL.
Oxenden Farm
Berwick Manor Farm
LYMPNE
ALDER COTTS.
BERWICK
ISIS CL.
OCTAVIAN DR.
Shepmead
LONDON ROAD
Court Wood
Oathill Cottages
Shipway Cross
THE RIDGEWAY
LANE
Prim. Sch.
ROAD
ALDINGTON
135
Shepway Cross
Hythe
CT21
ROAD
Vic.
LYMPNE HILL
Shepway
OLD LONDON RD.
Lympne Park Wood
West Hythe
West Hythe Water Works
THE ROUGHS
ST. MARY'S ROAD
West Hythe Bridge
Nursery
ROYAL ROAD
MILITARY ROAD
RIVERSIDE IND. EST.
CANAL
WOODLAND RISE
WEST HYTHE
BURMARSH
ELM CT.
34
GREBE CRES.
DOVE CL.
MARTIN'S WY.
MEADOW WAY
PEREGRINE CL.
OAKLANDS COTTS.
PRINCE OF WALES RESIDENTIAL PARK
Rose Cottage
Pipes Arm
WILLOW TREE FARM
BLUEWATER

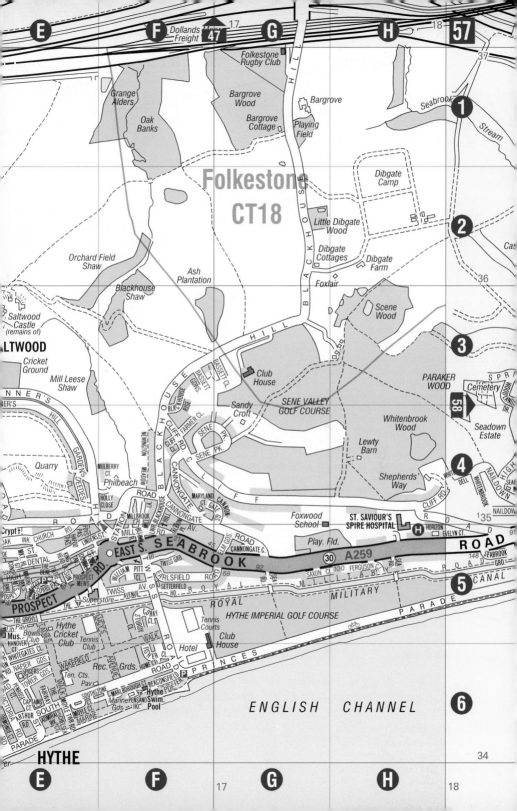

17

37

1

Folkestone CT18

Grange Alders

Oak Banks

Bargrove Wood

Bargrove

Bargrove Cottage

Playing Field

Folkestone Rugby Club

Seabrook

Stream

Dibgate Camp

2

Little Dibgate Wood

Cas

36

Orchard Field Shaw

Ash Plantation

Blackhouse Shaw

Dibgate Cottages

Dibgate Farm

Foxlair

Scene Wood

Saltwood Castle (remains of)

LTWOOD

Cricket Ground

Mill Leese Shaw

3

Club House

Sandy Croft

SENE VALLEY GOLF COURSE

PARAKER WOOD

Cemetery

58

Seadown Estate

BASSETT CL

BASSETT

BLACKHOUSE RISE

GUNS

CLIFF RD.

FARMER CL.

CLIFF CL.

SENE PK.

SENE PK.

Quarry

Philbeach

MULBERRY CT.

HOLLY CLOSE

Road

BLACKHOUSE

CANNONGATE

Whitenbrook Wood

Lewty Barn

Shepherds' Way

4

WHITE DELL

WHITENBROOK

NAILDOWN

SEA

135

NAILDOWN

MARYLAND CT.

CANNON

CANNONGATE

MILLBROOK

CLIFF

CLIFF RD.

ROAD

Foxwood School

ST. SAVIOUR'S SPIRE HOSPITAL

Play. Fld.

H HORIZON

EVELYN CT.

STATION

MILL

BLACKHOUSE

FITZ

THORN

GREY AV.

ROAD

CANNONGATE C.

ROAD

ROAD

Crypt†

East S. **SEABROOK**

30 A259

SEABROOK GRO

148

PROSPECT MEWS

WILLIAM PITT CL.

TWISS GRO.

EARLSFIELD RD.

SETTERFIELD HO.

SAXON CL

100 FERGUSON

MILITARY

ROAD

5

CANAL

DENTAL

THE DENE

Superstore

TWISS AVENUE

COBBY CL.

STURDY CL.

ROYAL

AVE.

PROSPECT RD.

PROSPECT

ROYAL

MILITARY

PARADE

HYTHE IMPERIAL GOLF COURSE

Hythe Cricket Club

Tennis Club

Tennis Courts

Club House

Hotel

PRINCES

ROAD

Lib Pav.

Mus.

Bowls Club

HANOVER CT.

WHITEGATES CL.

NAPIER GDS.

SPICERS GDS.

TOWER GDS.

WALK

LUCY'S CL.

Rec. Grds.

FISHER RD.

Ten. Cts. Pav.

HUME CT.

ROAD

WAKEFIELD

PENS

MOYLE CL.

MARINE

PDE

PARADE

SOUTH

ARTHUR RD.

VICTORIA RD.

CAPTAINS

FAIRWAY

PRINCES

MARLBOROUGH CT. BEACONSFIE

Marine Gds.

PENSAND HO.

Hythe Swim. Pool

P PDE

E N G L I S H   C H A N N E L

6

34

FOLKESTONE

37

EAST WEAR BAY

ello Tower
No.3

Pav.

❶

❷

36

❸

❹

¹35

C H A N N E L

❺

❻

34

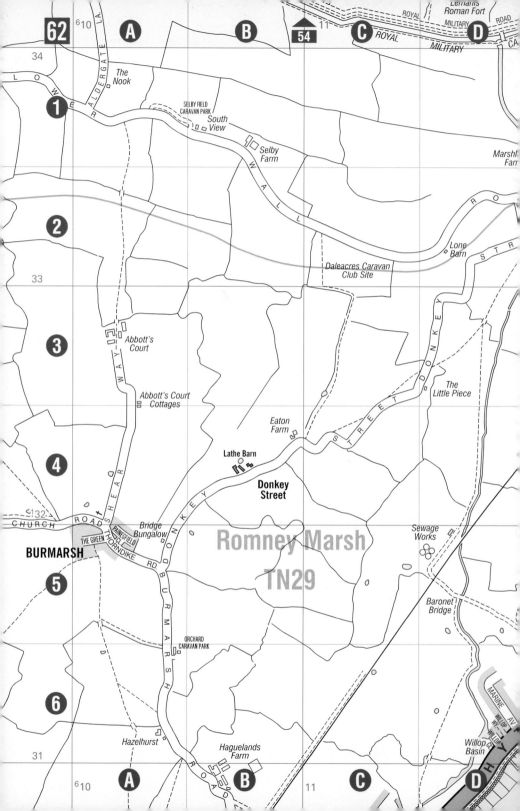

A　　　**B**　　⌂ 54　　11　　**C** ROYAL MILITARY　　**D**

34

Lemans Roman Fort

ROYAL MILITARY ROAD

CA

1 LOWER

ALDERGATE LA

The Nook

SELBY FIELD CARAVAN PARK

South View

Selby Farm

2 WALL

33

Marsh Farm

Lone Barn

Daleacres Caravan Club Site

STR

3

WAY

Abbott's Court

Abbott's Court Cottages

DONKEY STREET

The Little Piece

4

SHEAR

Eaton Farm

Lathe Barn

Donkey Street

DONKEY

ⁿ132

CHURCH ROAD

BURMARSH

The Green

PANESFIELD CL

THORNDIKE RD

Bridge Bungalow

Romney Marsh

Sewage Works

5 BURMARSH

BURMARSH

TN29

Baronet Bridge

ORCHARD CARAVAN PARK

6

ROAD

MARINE AV

WILLOP

WILLOP

HY

Hazelhurst

Haguelands Farm

Willop Basin

A　　⁶10　　**B**　　11　　**C**　　**D**

ENGLISH CHANNEL

Hythe
CT21

PALMARSH

HYTHE
RANGES

Danger
Area

Martello
Tower no. 19

BEACH BANK
CARAVAN SITE

Botolph's
Bridge

Stonereach
Bridge

Dykeside
Farm

Hopelands
Farm

Cinderella
Farm

The Pebbles

Rose
Cottage

Solway
Nursery

Willop
(Oaks Arm)

Sewer

Willop Sewer (Gill's Pipes Arm)

BURMARSH

Sewage
Works

Redoubt
Sailing Club

Rec. Grd.

Palmarsh
Prim. Sch.

Willow Tree Farm

Prince of Wales
Residential Park

BLUEWATER
CARAVAN PK.

Oaklands
Cotts.

ELM CT.

RIVERSIDE
IND. EST.

Nursery

ROYAL

ROYAL MILITARY ROAD

WOODLAND RD.

ROAD

HYTHE

BURMARSH ROAD

Fort
Lodge

River
Ho.

Depot

Wall

Dymchurch
Redoubt

Hythe and Dymchurch Railway

DYMCHURCH ROAD

ROAD

A259

NEW BEACH
HOLIDAY PARK

EASTFLEET
CARAVAN PARK

A259

Dymchurch

CRIMOND
AV.

BEVERLEY
GDNS.

BEACH R.

DENHAM CL.

LIVINGSTONE CL.

WOODLAND WY.

BROCKMAN CRES.

REDOUBT WAY

LAND WY.

BRIDGE ROAD

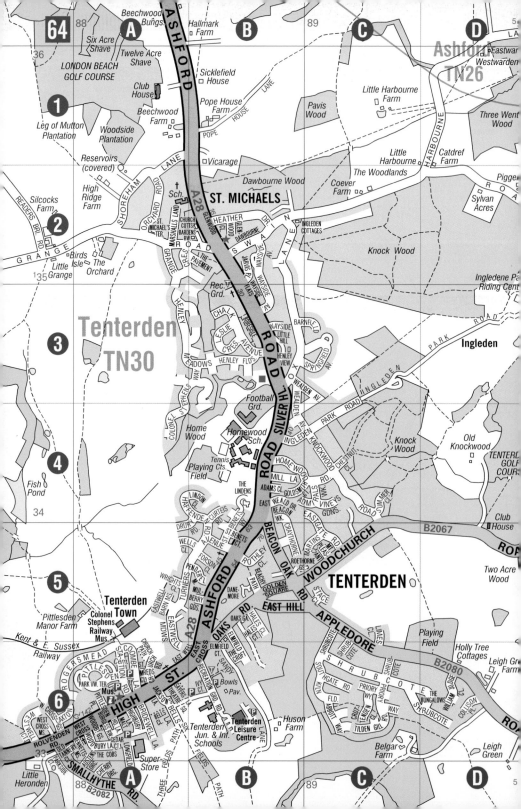

INDEX

Including Streets, Places & Areas, Hospitals etc., Industrial Estates,
Selected Flats & Walkways, Service Areas, Stations and Selected Places of Interest.

HOW TO USE THIS INDEX

1. Each street name is followed by its Postcode District, then by its Locality abbreviation(s) and then by its map reference;
e.g. **Abbey Rd.** CT15: Dover . . . .2D **26** is in the CT15 Postcode District and the Dover Locality and is to be found in square 2D on page **26**.
The page number is shown in bold type.

2. A strict alphabetical order is followed in which Av., Rd., St., etc. (though abbreviated) are read in full and as part of the street name;
e.g. **Green Flds. La.** appears after **Greenfields** but before **Greengates**

3. Streets and a selection of flats and walkways that cannot be shown on the mapping, appear in the index with the thoroughfare to which they are
connected shown in brackets; e.g. **Ackerley Ct.** TN23: Ashf . . . .1D **38** (off Stanhope Sq.)

4. Addresses that are in more than one part are referred to as not continuous.

5. Places and areas are shown in the index in BLUE TYPE and the map reference is to the actual map square in which the town centre or area is
located and not to the place name shown on the map; e.g. **BRABOURNE LEES** 2D **42**

6. An example of a selected place of interest is **Deal Castle** 6H **9**

7. An example of a station is **Deal Station (Rail)** 5G **9**

8. Service Areas are shown in the index in BOLD CAPITAL TYPE; e.g. **STOP 24 SERVICE AREA** 6G **45**

9. An example of a Hospital, Hospice or selected Healthcare facility is **BUCKLAND HOSPITAL** 2A **28**

10. Map references for entries that appear on large scale pages **4-7** are shown first, with small scale map references shown in brackets;
e.g. **Alder Rd.** CT19: F'stone 1E **5** (1A **60**)

GENERAL ABBREVIATIONS

All. : Alley	**Gdns.** : Gardens	**Pk.** : Park
App. : Approach	**Ga.** : Gate	**Pas.** : Passage
Av. : Avenue	**Gt.** : Great	**Pl.** : Place
Bri. : Bridge	**Grn.** : Green	**Prom.** : Promenade
Bldgs. : Buildings	**Gro.** : Grove	**Res.** : Residential
Bungs. : Bungalows	**Hgts.** : Heights	**Ri.** : Rise
Bus. : Business	**Ho.** : House	**Rd.** : Road
Cvn. : Caravan	**Ho's.** : Houses	**Rdbt.** : Roundabout
Cen. : Centre	**Ind.** : Industrial	**Shop.** : Shopping
Chu. : Church	**Info.** : Information	**Sth.** : South
Cl. : Close	**La.** : Lane	**Sq.** : Square
Comn. : Common	**Lit.** : Little	**Sta.** : Station
Cnr. : Corner	**Lwr.** : Lower	**St.** : Street
Cott. : Cottage	**Mnr.** : Manor	**Ter.** : Terrace
Cotts. : Cottages	**Mans.** : Mansions	**Twr.** : Tower
Ct. : Court	**Mkt.** : Market	**Trad.** : Trading
Cres. : Crescent	**Mdw.** : Meadow	**Up.** : Upper
Dr. : Drive	**Mdws.** : Meadows	**Va.** : Vale
E. : East	**M.** : Mews	**Vw.** : View
Ent. : Enterprise	**Mt.** : Mount	**Vs.** : Villas
Est. : Estate	**Mus.** : Museum	**Vis.** : Visitors
Fld. : Field	**Nth.** : North	**Wlk.** : Walk
Flds. : Fields	**No.** : Number	**W.** : West
Gdn. : Garden	**Pde.** : Parade	**Yd.** : Yard

LOCALITY ABBREVIATIONS

Acr : **Acrise**	Hackl : **Hacklinge**	Ripp : **Ripple**
Aldtn : **Aldington**	H'nge : **Hawkinge**	St Marg : **St Margarets-at-Cliffe**
Alk : **Alkham**	H Hald : **High Halden**	St Mic : **St Michaels**
Ashf : **Ashford**	Hin : **Hinxhill**	Salt : **Saltwood**
Bett : **Betteshanger**	Hoth : **Hothfield**	S'gte : **Sandgate**
Bou A : **Boughton Aluph**	Hou : **Hougham**	S'lng : **Sandling**
Bou L : **Boughton Lees**	Hythe : **Hythe**	S'ndge : **Sellindge**
Bra L : **Brabourne Lees**	Kenn : **Kennington**	Svgtn : **Sevington**
Brook : **Brook**	Kgdn : **Kingsdown**	Shad : **Shadoxhurst**
Burm : **Burmarsh**	Kgnt : **Kingsnorth**	Shol : **Sholden**
Cap F : **Capel-le-Ferne**	L Mon : **Little Mongeham**	Sme : **Smeeth**
Chu H : **Church Hougham**	Lyd'n : **Lydden**	Stanf : **Stanford**
Cold : **Coldred**	Lym'ge : **Lyminge**	Stu X : **Stubbs Cross**
Deal : **Deal**	Lymp : **Lympne**	Sutt : **Sutton**
D'sole : **Densole**	Mart : **Martin**	S'fld : **Swingfield**
Dover : **Dover**	Mart M : **Martin Mill**	Temp E : **Temple Ewell**
Drel : **Drellingore**	Mers : **Mersham**	Tent : **Tenterden**
Dym : **Dymchurch**	M Hor : **Monks Horton**	Walm : **Walmer**
E Bra : **East Brabourne**	N'grn : **Newingreen**	W Bra : **West Brabourne**
E Lan : **East Langdon**	N'tn : **Newington**	W Hou : **West Hougham**
E'well : **Eastwell**	N'bne : **Northbourne**	W Hyt : **West Hythe**
Elham : **Elham**	O'nge : **Ottinge**	W Lan : **West Langdon**
Etch'l : **Etchinghill**	P'wth : **Paddlesworth**	Wnhgr : **Westenhanger**
Ewe M : **Ewell Minnis**	Ped : **Pedlinge**	Westw : **Westwell**
Fin : **Finglesham**	Peene : **Peene**	Whitf : **Whitfield**
F'stone : **Folkestone**	Pine : **Pineham**	W'boro : **Willesborough**
Gt Cha : **Great Chart**	Post : **Postling**	Worth : **Worth**
Gt Mon : **Great Mongeham**	R Min : **Rhodes Minnis**	Wye : **Wye**
Gus : **Guston**	R'wld : **Ringwould**	

A

Abbey Cl. CT14: Deal 6E **9**
Abbey Rd. CT15: Dover 2D **26**
   CT15: W Lan, Whitf 1C **16**
   CT16: Temp E 5F **15**
   CT17: Dover 2D **26**
Abbey Way TN24: W'boro 3C **36**
Abbots, The CT17: Dover 4B **6** (3C **28**)
Abbots Wlk. TN25: Wye 1G **33**
Abbott Cl. CT20: F'stone 2H **5**
Abbott Rd. CT20: F'stone 2H **5** (1C **60**)
Abbott Way TN30: Tent 6C **64**
Academy La. CT19: F'stone 6H **49**
Ackerley Ct. TN23: Ashf 1D **38**
                  (off Stanhope Sq.)
Acorn Cl. CT18: H'nge 1A **50**
   TN23: Kgnt 4G **39**
Acre, The CT16: Whitf 1H **15**
Acre Ct. CT17: Dover 3C **6** (3C **28**)
ACRISE 2C **22**
Adams Cl. TN30: Tent 4B **64**
Adams Dr. TN24: Ashf 5H **35**
Addelam Cl. CT14: Deal 1E **11**
Addelam Rd. CT14: Deal 1E **11**
Adisham Gdns. TN23: Ashf 1D **38**
Admirals Wlk. CT21: Hythe 6E **57**
   TN30: Tent 4C **64**
Admiralty M. CT14: Walm 1H **11**
Adrian St. CT17: Dover 6E **7** (4D **28**)
Aerodrome Rd. CT18: H'nge, P'wth . . .1D **48**
Ainsdale Cl. CT19: F'stone 6H **49**
Alamein Cl. CT15: Gus 1F **29**
Albany Ho. CT17: Dover 5E **7**
Albany Pl. CT17: Dover 5E **7** (4D **28**)
Albany Rd. CT18: Cap F 4F **51**
Albatross Lodge CT16: Dover 1B **28**
Albemarle Rd. TN24: W'boro 5A **36**
Alberta Cl. CT16: Dover 6B **16**
Albert Costain Ct. CT20: F'stone 3F **5**
Albert La. CT21: Hythe 6D **56**
Albert Rd. CT14: Deal 5G **9**
   CT16: Dover 2D **6** (2D **28**)
   CT18: Cap F 4G **51**
   CT19: F'stone 1F **5** (1B **60**)
   CT21: Hythe 6D **56**
   TN24: Ashf 2B **4** (2F **35**)
Albion Mews Rd. CT20: F'stone 5F **5** (3B **60**)
Albion Pl. CT21: Hythe 5F **57**
   TN24: W'boro 6A **36**
Albion Rd. CT14: Deal 3H **9**
   CT19: F'stone 1G **5** (1B **60**)
Albion Vs. CT20: F'stone 5G **5** (3B **60**)
Alder Cotts. CT21: Lymp 4E **55**
Aldergate La. CT21: W Hyt 6A **54**
Alder Ho. TN23: Ashf 4D **34**
Alderney Way TN24: Kenn 4G **31**
Alder Rd. CT19: F'stone 1E **5** (1A **60**)
Aldington Rd. CT21: Lymp 4A **54**
Alec Pemble Cl. TN24: Kenn 6A **32**
Alexandra Corniche
   CT21: F'stone, Hythe, S'gte 4B **58**
Alexandra Ct. CT21: Hythe 6C **56**
Alexandra Dr. CT14: Deal 2D **10**
Alexandra Gdns. CT20: F'stone 5G **5** (3B **60**)
Alexandra Pl. CT17: Dover 1B **6** (2C **28**)
Alexandra Rd. CT14: Kgdn 2G **13**
   CT14: Walm 3H **11**
   CT18: Cap F 3F **51**
Alexandra St. CT19: F'stone 1H **5** (1C **60**)
Alexandra Ter. TN25: Mers 4F **41**
Alfred Rd. CT16: Dover 1B **28**
   TN24: Ashf 6H **35**
Alfred Row CT14: Deal 4H **9**
Alfred Sq. CT14: Deal 4H **9**
Alison Cl. CT16: Whitf 3A **16**
Alison Cres. CT16: Whitf 2A **16**
ALKHAM 2H **25**
Alkham Rd. CT15: Temp E 6D **14**
   CT16: Temp E 6D **14**
Alkham Valley Rd. CT15: Alk, Drel 3G **25**
   CT18: Drel, F'stone 3A **50**
Allenby Av. CT14: Deal 6F **9**
Allendale St. CT19: F'stone 1F **5** (1B **60**)
Allen Fld. TN23: Ashf 5D **34**
Alma Rd. CT20: F'stone 2D **58**
Almond Cl. TN25: Kenn 6D **30**
Alsops Rd. TN24: W'boro 6A **36**

American Garden, The 2C **56**
AMF Bowling
   Ashford 4D **4** (3G **35**)
Anchor La. CT14: Deal 5G **9**
Angel Hgts. CT18: H'nge 2E **49**
Angus Dr. TN24: Kenn 4G **31**
Anselm Rd. CT17: Dover 3A **28**
Anstee Rd. CT17: Dover 2B **6** (2C **28**)
Antelope Cl. CT16: Whitf 4A **16**
Antonius Ct. TN23: Kgnt 2D **38**
Anzio Cres. CT15: Gus 1E **29**
Apple Cl. CT18: H'nge 1H **49**
Appledore Cres. CT19: F'stone 6D **48**
Appledore Rd. TN30: Tent 5C **64**
Approach Rd. CT17: Dover 5A **28**
Apsley St. TN23: Ashf 4A **4** (3F **35**)
Aragon Cl. TN23: Ashf 6C **34**
Archcliffe Rd. CT17: Dover 6C **28**
Archer Rd. CT19: F'stone 1G **5** (1B **60**)
Archer's Ct. Rd. CT16: Whitf 3A **16**
Archery Sq. CT14: Walm 2H **11**
                  (not continuous)
Arcon Cl. TN23: Ashf 6E **35**
Arcon Rd. TN23: Ashf 6E **35**
Arden Dr. TN24: Ashf 1D **4** (2G **35**)
Ardent Av. CT14: Walm 1G **11**
Ardent Rd. CT16: Whitf 4A **16**
Argyll Ct. CT14: Walm 1H **11**
Ark La. CT14: Deal 4G **9**
Arlington TN23: Ashf 4D **34**
Armourer's Wlk. CT16: Dover 6A **16**
Arthur Rd. CT14: Deal 2E **11**
   CT21: Hythe 6E **57**
Arthur St. CT19: F'stone 1H **5** (1C **60**)
Ashborne Cl. TN24: Kenn 5H **31**
Ashburton Cl. TN24: W'boro 3A **36**
Ash Cl. CT17: Dover 1H **27**
   TN23: Ashf 3C **34**
Ashdale Pl. TN23: Ashf 3C **4**
Ashdown Ct. TN24: Ashf 2C **4** (2G **35**)
Ashen Tree La. CT16: Dover 4F **7** (3E **29**)
ASHFORD 3B **4** (3F **35**)
Ashford Bus. Pk. TN24: Svgtn 1C **40**
Ashford Bus. Point TN24: Ashf 2B **40**
Ashford Ct. TN24: Ashf 1B **4** (2F **35**)
Ashford Designer Outlet TN24: Ashf . . .6G **35**
Ashford Golf Course 4D **30**
Ashford International Station (Rail)
                   6C **4** (4G **35**)
Ashford Mus. 3B **4**
Ashford Retail Pk. TN24: Svgtn 1C **40**
Ashford Rd. CT18: N'tn, Peene 5C **46**
   CT21: N'grn, Post, Salt, S'lng 2F **55**
   TN23: Ashf, Kgnt 2E **39**
   TN23: Gt Cha 5A **34**
   TN25: S'ndge 1C **54**
                   (Barrow Hill)
   TN25: S'ndge 6G **43**
                   (Stone Hill)
   TN30: St Mic 1A **64**
   TN30: Tent 5B **64**
Ashford Trade Cen. TN24: Svgtn 1B **40**
Ash Gro. CT15: St Marg 3D **18**
Ashgrove TN25: Ashf 6D **30**
Ashley Av. CT19: F'stone 1E **59**
Ashley Ho. CT19: F'stone 1E **59**
Ashley Mill Cotts. *CT19: F'stone* 6E **49**
                  (off Ashley Av.)
Ash Mdw. TN24: W'boro 6B **36**
Ashton Cl. TN24: Gt Mon 1B **10**
Ash Tree Rd. CT19: F'stone 1H **5** (1C **60**)
Askes Ct. TN23: Ashf 5B **34**
Aspen Dr. CT16: Whitf 4A **16**
   TN23: Ashf 2B **34**
Aspen Ho. CT20: F'stone 5G **5** (3B **60**)
Astley Av. CT16: Dover 1C **6** (1C **28**)
Astley Ct. CT16: Dover 1C **6**
Astor Av. CT17: Dover 4A **6** (4B **28**)
Astor Dr. CT14: Deal 6G **9**
Astor Theatre Arts Centre, The 5H **9**
Astrid Rd. CT14: Walm 3E **11**
Athelstan Pl. CT14: Deal 3G **9**
Athelstan Rd. CT19: F'stone 6B **50**
Athol Rd. TN23: Ashf 6D **34**
Athol Ter. CT16: Dover 3F **29**
Atkinson Rd. CT18: H'nge 2F **49**
Atkinson Wlk. TN24: Kenn 6B **32**
Auckland Cres. CT16: Dover 6C **16**

Auden Way CT17: Dover 4A **6** (3B **28**)
Audley Rd. CT20: F'stone 2F **59**
Augusta Gdns. CT20: F'stone 3A **60**
Augustus Wlk. TN23: Kgnt 2D **38**
Aurelius Cl. TN23: Kgnt 3E **39**
Austens Orchard TN30: Tent 6A **64**
Austin Rd. TN23: Ashf 1F **39**
Avenue, The CT14: Deal 4G **9**
   CT14: Kgdn 2G **13**
   CT15: St Marg 3D **18**
   CT16: Temp E 4F **15**
   CT21: Hythe 5E **57**
Avenue Rd. CT16: Dover 1C **6** (2C **28**)
Avereng Gdns. CT19: F'stone 1H **59**
Avereng Rd. CT19: F'stone 1H **59**
Avondale Rd. CT18: Cap F 3G **51**
Avon Ho. CT20: F'stone 6E **5** (3A **60**)
AYCLIFF 6B **28**
Aylesbury Rd. TN25: Kenn 4F **31**
Aylesford Pl. TN24: W'boro 6A **36**
Ayrshire Cl. TN24: Kenn 4G **31**

B

Back La. CT15: Hou, W Hou 5B **26**
Back Rd. W. CT16: Dover 3F **29**
Back St. CT14: R'wld 2D **12**
   CT19: F'stone 4H **5** (2C **60**)
Badgers Bri. CT18: Etch'l 1F **47**
Badgers Den TN23: Ashf 6B **34**
Badgers Oak TN23: Ashf 5B **34**
Badgers Ri. CT14: Walm 5G **11**
   CT17: Dover 6F **15**
Badlesmere Cl. TN23: Ashf 1C **38**
Bad Munstereifel Rd. TN23: Ashf 2F **39**
   TN24: Ashf, Svgtn, W'boro 2F **39**
Baileys Fld. TN23: Ashf 4D **34**
Bail Steps *CT20: F'stone* 4H **5**
             (off The Old High St.)
Baker Rd. CT19: F'stone 1E **59**
Baldric Rd. CT20: F'stone 2F **59**
Baldwin Ter. CT19: F'stone 1G **5** (1C **60**)
Balfour Ct. CT20: F'stone 4G **59**
Balfour Ho. CT16: Dover 1C **6**
Balfour Rd. CT14: Walm 3G **11**
   CT16: Dover 1B **6** (2C **28**)
Ball La. TN25: Kenn 4A **32**
                  (not continuous)
Balmoral Rd. CT14: Kgdn 1G **13**
Bamford Way CT14: Deal 1G **11**
Bank Ct. CT16: Dover 3C **6**
Bank Rd. TN25: Mers 6E **41**
Banks Rd. TN23: Ashf 6E **35**
Bank St. CT21: Hythe 5E **57**
   TN23: Ashf 4B **4** (3F **35**)
Bannatyne's Health Club
   Ashford 1G **35**
Bardens Row TN30: St Mic 2A **64**
Bargates TN23: Ashf 1C **38**
Barley Cl. CT15: Mart M 5A **12**
Barley Ct. TN23: Ashf 6E **35**
Barley Mow Vw. TN23: Ashf 1D **34**
Barley Way TN23: Kgnt 2C **38**
Barnberry Cl. TN23: Ashf 5C **34**
Barnett Fld. TN23: Ashf 5D **34**
Barnfield TN30: St Mic 3B **64**
Barnfield Rd. CT19: F'stone 6A **50**
Barnhurst La. CT18: H'nge 6G **23**
Barn Platt TN23: Ashf 5E **35**
Barn Tye Cl. CT15: Gus 3E **17**
Barntye Rd. CT15: Gus 4D **16**
Barrack Hill CT21: Hythe 5C **56**
Barrey Rd. TN24: Svgtn 1C **40**
BARROW HILL 3A **4** (2E **35**)
BARROWHILL 5B **44**
Barrow Hill TN23: Ashf 3A **4** (3F **35**)
   TN25: S'ndge 5B **44**
Barrow Hill Cotts. TN23: Ashf 3A **4** (2E **35**)
Barrow Hill Pl. TN23: Ashf 2A **4** (2E **35**)
Barrow Hill Ri. TN25: S'ndge 6B **44**
Barrow Hill Ter. TN23: Ashf 2A **4**
Bartholomew Cl. CT21: Hythe 4D **56**
Bartholomew La. CT21: Hythe 4C **56**
Bartholomew St. CT16: Dover 2C **6** (2C **28**)
   CT21: Hythe 5D **56**
Bartlets La. TN23: Gt Cha 3A **38**
Barton Fld. CT18: Lym'ge 4D **20**
Barton Path CT16: Dover 1B **6** (1C **28**)
Barton Rd. CT16: Dover 1B **6** (1C **28**)

Barton Vw. Ter. CT17: Dover 1B 6 (2C 28)
Barwick Rd. CT17: Dover 2H 27
Barwick Rd. Ind. Est. CT17: Dover 2H 27
Baskerville TN24: Ashf 1B 4 (2F 35)
Bassett Cl. CT21: Hythe 3G 57
Bassett Gdns. CT21: Hythe 3F 57
Bastion Rd. CT17: Dover 6C 6 (4C 28)
Bath Ct. CT20: F'stone 4H 59
Bath M. TN24: W'boro 1A 40
Bath Rd. TN24: W'boro 1A 40
Bathurst Rd. CT20: F'stone 2F 59
Battery Point CT21: Hythe 5B 58
Battle of Britain Flats CT17: Dover 5E 7
Battle of Britain Memorial, The 4F 51
Baxendale Ct. TN24: Ashf 6H 35
Bay Cotts. CT15: St Marg 3F 19
Bay Hill CT15: St Marg 4E 19
Bay Hill Cl. CT15: St Marg 4E 19
Bayle, The CT20: F'stone 5H 5 (3C 60)
Bayle Ct. CT20: F'stone 5H 5 (3C 60)
Bayle St. CT20: F'stone 4H 5 (2C 60)
Bay Vw. CT20: S'gte 4C 58
Bayview Rd. CT14: Kgdn 3G 13
Beach, The CT14: Walm 2H 11
Beach Bank Caravan Site CT21: Hythe 2G 63
BEACHBOROUGH .4F 47
Beachborough Rd. CT19: F'stone 1G 59
Beach Ct. CT14: Deal 1D 10
CT14: Walm 3H 11
Beach Flats CT21: Hythe 5D 56
Beach Marine CT20: S'gte 4F 59
Beach Rd. CT15: St Marg 6E 19
TN29: Dym 5E 63
Beach St. CT14: Deal 4H 9
CT20: F'stone 4H 5 (3C 60)
Beachy Path TN30: Tent 5B 64
Beacon Hill CT14: L Mon 2A 10
Beacon Oak Rd. TN30: Tent 5B 64
Beaconsfield Rd. CT16: Dover 1C 6 (2C 28)
Beaconsfield Rd. CT14: Deal 6H 9
CT16: Dover 2B 6 (2C 28)
Beaconsfield Ter. CT21: Hythe 6F 57
Beacon Ter. CT21: Hythe 5B 58
Beacon Wlk. TN30: Tent 4B 64
Beacon Way CT21: Lymp 4D 54
Bean Cl. TN23: Gt Cha 4A 34
Bear's End Ho. TN23: Ashf 6B 4 (5F 35)
Beatrice Hills Cl. TN24: Kenn 6A 32
Beatrice Rd. CT18: Cap F 3G 51
Beatty Cl. CT19: F'stone 5C 50
Beatty Rd. CT19: F'stone 5B 50
Beauchamp Av. CT14: Deal 2E 11
Beauchamp Cl. TN24: Kenn 6A 32
Beaufoy Rd. CT17: Dover 2A 28
Beaufoy Ter. CT17: Dover 2H 27
Beauxfield CT16: Whitf 1A 16
BEAVER 6E 35
Beaver Ct. TN23: Ashf 6E 35
Beaver Ind. Est. TN23: Ashf 6F 35
Beaver La. TN23: Ashf 3C 34
(Chart Rd.)
TN23: Ashf 5C 34
(Oakleigh Ho.)
Beaver Rd. TN23: Ashf 6C 4 (6F 35)
Beazley Ct. TN24: Ashf 6H 35
Becket Ct. CT14: Deal 3G 9
Beckley Pl. TN25: Stanf 5F 45
Beckwith Grn. CT20: F'stone 2D 58
Bede Ho. CT14: Deal 3H 9
Bedford Vs. TN25: Sme 2D 42
Bedingfield Way CT18: Lym'ge 4D 20
Beech Cl. CT19: F'stone 1A 60
Beech Dr. TN26: Hoth 1D 30
Beecholme Dr. TN24: Kenn 6G 31
Beech Vs. CT4: Elham 5H 23
Beechwood Av. CT14: Deal 6G 9
Beechwood Cl. CT16: Whitf 1A 16
Beechwood Ct. CT14: Deal 6G 9
CT16: Dover 5G 15
Belcaire Cl. CT21: Lymp 4E 55
Belgrave Ho. CT17: Dover 6A 6 (4B 28)
Belgrave Rd. CT17: Dover 6A 6 (4B 28)
Belinda Ct. CT19: F'stone 6H 49
Bell Chapel Cl. TN23: Kgnt 3G 39
Bellevue St. CT20: F'stone 3G 5 (6B 60)
Bell Field TN25: Mers 4F 41
Bell Inn Rd. CT21: Hythe 5F 57
Bells Ct. TN30: Tent 6A 64
Bells La. TN30: Tent 6A 64

Belmont CT14: Walm 4F 11
Belmont Pl. TN23: Ashf 6H 35
(not continuous)
Belmont Rd. TN24: Kenn 5H 31
Belmore Pk. TN24: Ashf 1A 4 (2F 35)
Belsey Ct. CT15: Ewe M 5A 14
Beltex Pl. TN25: Mers 5H 39
Bench St. CT16: Dover 5F 7 (4D 28)
Bennett Ct. CT20: F'stone 4H 5
Bennetts M. TN30: Tent 6A 64
Benson Cl. CT18: H'nge 1F 49
Benson La. CT18: H'nge 1F 49
Bensted TN23: Ashf 2D 38
Bentley Rd. TN24: W'boro 6A 36
Beresford Rd. CT15: St Marg 6D 12
CT17: Dover 6G 15
Berkeley Ct. CT19: F'stone 6G 49
Berries, The CT18: H'nge 6H 23
Berwick La. CT21: Lymp 4E 55
Bethersden Rd. TN26: Hoth 2C 30
TN26: Shad 5C 38
Betteshanger Bus. Pk. CT14: Fin 4A 8
Betty Shelvey Ct. CT14: Deal 6G 9
(off Finch M.)
Beulah Vs. CT17: Dover 6A 16
Bevan Cl. CT14: Deal 3F 11
Beverley Gdns. TN29: Dym 5E 63
Bewsbury Cres. CT16: Whitf 2H 15
Bewsbury Cross La. CT16: Whitf 2H 15
Biggin St. CT16: Dover 4D 6 (3D 28)
(not continuous)
Biggins Wood Rd. CT19: F'stone 6D 48
Billington Gdns. TN24: Kenn 5A 32
Billington Gro. TN24: W'boro 5A 36
Bindon Blood Rd. CT16: Whitf 4A 16
Birch Cl. TN24: W'boro 3A 36
Birchett TN23: Ashf 4C 34
Birch Way CT21: Hythe 6B 56
Birch Wood Ri. CT17: Dover 6C 6 (4C 28)
Birdwood Av. CT14: Deal 6E 9
Birkdale Dr. CT19: F'stone 6G 49
Birling Rd. TN24: Ashf 3H 35
Bishops Cl. CT18: H'nge 2G 49
Bishops Grn. TN23: Ashf 6B 34
Bishopswood TN23: Kgnt 4G 39
Bittern Cl. CT18: H'nge 2G 49
Black Bull Rd. CT19: F'stone 2F 5 (1B 60)
Blackdown Dr. TN24: Ashf 1B 4 (1F 35)
Black Hill CT14: Ripp 3A 10
Blackhouse Hill CT18: N'trn 3G 07
CT21: Hythe, N'trn 4F 57
Blackhouse Ri. CT21: Hythe 4F 57
Blackthorn Way TN23: Kgnt 4G 39
Blackwall Rd. TN24: W'boro 3D 36
TN25: Hin, W'boro 3D 36
Blackwall Rd. Nth. TN24: W'boro 3C 36
Blackwall Rd. Sth. TN24: W'boro 3C 36
Blake Cl. CT14: Walm 5F 11
Blake Ct. TN24: W'boro 5B 36
Bland Dr. CT18: H'nge 6A 24
Blenheim Dr. CT16: Dover 4H 15
CT18: H'nge 1G 49
Blenheim Pl. CT20: F'stone 3F 59
Blenheim Rd. CT14: Deal 6H 9
Bleriot Memorial 2H 7 (2F 29)
Blindgrooms La. TN26: Shad 6A 38
Blindhouse La. TN25: M Hor 2D 44
Blind La. TN25: Mers 3E 41
Bloomsbury Way TN24: Kenn 4F 31
Blossom La. TN25: Mers 6C 30
Bluebell Cl. TN23: Kgnt 3F 39
Bluebell Rd. TN23: Kgnt 3F 39
Blue Fld. TN23: Ashf 5A 34
Blue Ho. La. CT21: Salt 6D 46
Blue Line La. TN24: Ashf 2A 4 (2F 35)
Bluewater Caravan Pk. CT21: Hythe 1H 63
Blythe Ct. CT21: Hythe 5F 57
(off Prospect Rd.)
Bockham La. TN25: W Bra 6F 37
BOCKHANGER 5G 31
Bockhanger Ct. TN24: Kenn 6H 31
Bockhanger La. TN24: Kenn 6G 31
Bodenham Rd. CT20: F'stone 3G 59
Bodiam Av. TN25: Mers 5A 40
Bolton Rd. CT19: F'stone 2G 5 (1B 60)
Bond La. TN23: Kgnt 5E 39
Bond Rd. TN23: Ashf 5E 35
Bonsor Rd. CT19: F'stone 1E 5 (1B 60)
Boresisle TN30: St Mic 3B 64

Bornefields TN23: Ashf 6E 35
Boscombe Rd. CT19: F'stone 2E 5 (1A 60)
Bosney Banks CT15: Lyd'n 2B 14
Boston Cl. CT16: Dover 6B 16
BOTOLPH'S BRIDGE 2E 63
Botolph's Bri. Rd. CT21: W Hyt 2E 63
BOUGHTON LEES 1A 32
Boulevard, The TN24: Ashf 1B 40
Boulogne Ct. CT20: F'stone 4H 5
Boundary Rd. CT14: Kgdn 1H 13
CT21: Hythe 6C 56
Bournemouth Gdns. CT19: F'stone . . .2E 5 (1A 60)
Bournemouth Rd. CT19: F'stone . . .2E 5 (1A 60)
Bouverie M. CT20: F'stone 3A 60
Bouverie Pl. CT20: F'stone 5F 5 (3B 60)
Bouverie Pl. Shop. Cen.
CT20: F'stone 5F 5 (3B 60)
Bouverie Rd. W. CT20: F'stone 5E 5 (3G 59)
Bouverie Sq. CT20: F'stone 5F 5 (3B 60)
Bowden Cres. CT20: F'stone 1C 58
Bowen Rd. CT19: F'stone 1E 59
Bowens Fld. TN23: Ashf 6A 4 (4H 35)
Bower Cotts. TN25: Mers 3G 41
Bower Rd. TN25: Mers, Sme 3G 41
Bowles Well Gdns. CT19: F'stone 6D 50
(not continuous)
Bowling Grn. La. CT14: Deal 6F 9
Bowling Grn. Ter. CT17: Dover 5D 6 (4D 28)
Bowser Cl. CT14: Deal 1D 10
Boxley TN23: Ashf 5D 34
Boyke La. CT4: O'nge, R Min 1D 20
Boyne Rd. CT15: Mers 1E 19
Boys Hall Rd. TN24: Ashf, W'boro 6B 36
Brabner Ct. CT19: F'stone 5C 50
Brabourne Gdns. CT20: F'stone 2E 59
BRABOURNE LEES 2D 42
Bracken Cl. TN24: Kenn 5G 31
Bradbridge Grn. TN23: Ashf 5B 34
Bradfield Rd. TN25: Ashf 6F 31
Bradfoord Ct. CT20: F'stone 3F 5 (2B 60)
Bradley Rd. CT19: F'stone 1D 60
Bradstone Av. CT19: F'stone 2F 5 (1B 60)
Bradstone Ct. CT20: F'stone 3G 5
Bradstone New Rd. CT20: F'stone . . .3G 5 (2B 60)
Bradstone Rd. CT20: F'stone 3G 5 (2B 60)
Brady Rd. CT18: Lym'ge 6A 20
Bramble Cl. TN25: Wye 1F 33
Brambledown CT19: F'stone 2G 5 (1B 60)
Bramble Hill CT15: Hou 4H 25
Bramble La. TN25: Bou L, Wye 1F 33
Brambles Ct. Yd. CT14: Deal 2F 11
Bramble Wlk. TN23: Kgnt 5G 39
Brambley Cres. CT20: F'stone 6C 58
Bramley Cl. TN25: Bra L 1E 43
Bramley Cotts. TN25: Kenn 4C 32
Bramley Gdns. TN23: Ashf 1E 39
Bramling Ct. TN24: Kenn 6G 31
Branch St. CT16: Dover 2C 6 (2C 28)
Brassey Rd. CT16: Whitf 4A 16
Breadlands Cl. TN24: W'boro 5A 36
Breadlands Rd. TN24: W'boro 5B 36
Brecon Ri. TN24: Ashf 1F 35
Bredgar Cl. TN24: Ashf 1D 38
Brenchley Av. CT14: Deal 1D 10
Brenchley Cl. TN23: Ashf 1C 38
Brendon Dr. TN24: Ashf 1B 4 (1F 35)
Brentwood CT14: Deal 2D 38
Brewer's Hill CT20: S'gte 4D 58
Brewer St. CT14: Deal 5H 9
Briar Cl. CT17: Dover 1H 27
TN24: Kenn 5G 31
TN25: Wye 1F 33
Briar Cl. Bus. Pk. TN25: Wye 1F 33
Brickfield Cotts. TN25: Bou A 1D 32
Brickworks La. TN25: Brook 5F 33
Bridewell La. TN30: Tent 6A 64
Bridge Cl. CT21: Hythe 5C 56
Bridge Hill CT14: Hackl 3A 8
Bridgeman Ct. CT21: Hythe 5D 56
Bridge Rd. CT14: Deal 4H 9
TN23: Ashf 3D 34
TN25: Bra L 2D 42
Bridge Rd. Bus. Cen. TN23: Ashf 3D 34
Bridgeside CT14: Deal 5G 9
Bridge St. CT16: Dover 2C 6 (2C 28)
CT19: F'stone 1H 5 (1C 60)
TN25: Wye 1F 33
Bridle Way CT16: Whitf 2H 15
CT21: Hythe 4A 58

Bridleway La. TN23: Kgnt 3F 39
Brigadier Gdns. TN23: Ashf 1D 34
Brisley Cl. TN23: Kgnt 1B 38
Brisley Ct. TN23: Ashf, Kgnt 1B 38
Britannia La. TN23: Kgnt 2D 38
Britannia Rd. CT14: Deal 3H 9
Britten Cl. CT21: Hythe 4C 56
Broadacre CT15: Lyd'n 1B 14
Broadfield Cres. CT20: F'stone 2G 59
Broadfield Rd. CT20: F'stone 2G 59
Broadhembury Caravan & Camping Pk.
  TN26: Kgnt .6F 39
Broadhurst Dr. TN24: Kenn 4H 31
Broad La. CT14: Bett, Fin 4A 8
Broadmead TN23: Ashf 3C 34
Broadmead Rd.
  CT19: F'stone 3E 5 (2A 60)
BROADMEAD VILLAGE 6G 49
BROAD OAK 6E 41
Broadsole La. CT15: W Hou 6A 26
BROAD STREET
  CT18 . . . . .6E 21
  TN25 . . . . .1D 44
Broad St. CT14: Deal 5H 9
  CT18: Lym'ge 1D 46
Broadview CT20: F'stone 1C 58
Broadview Cl. TN25: Mers 5H 39
Broadviews CT21: Hythe 6F 57
  (off South Rd.)
Brockhill Country Pk. 3B 56
Brockhill Rd. CT21: Hythe 4D 56
Brockman Cres. TN29: Dym 4F 63
Brockman Rd. CT20: F'stone 4E 5 (2A 60)
Brompton Vs. CT15: Gus 3E 17
BROOK 6H 33
Brook Cl. CT21: Hythe 4B 58
Brooke Rd. TN24: Ashf 1A 4 (2F 35)
Brookfield Av. CT16: Dover 1B 28
Brookfield Ct. TN23: Ashf 5D 34
Brookfield Ind. Pk. TN23: Ashf 4D 34
Brookfield Pl. CT16: Dover 1B 28
Brookfield Rd. CT16: Dover 6A 16
  TN23: Ashf .4C 34
Brook La. TN25: S'ndge 3C 44
Brook La. Cotts. TN25: S'ndge 3C 44
Brookside CT16: Temp E 4E 15
Broomfield TN24: W'boro 5D 36
Broomfield Cres. CT19: F'stone 1E 59
Broomfield Rd. CT19: F'stone 1E 59
Broughton Ct. TN23: Ashf 4C 34
Browning Pl. CT19: F'stone 6C 50
Bruce Cl. CT14: Deal 1F 11
Brunswick Gdns. CT16: Dover 6B 16
Brunswick Ind. Cen. TN23: Ashf 3D 34
Brunswick Rd. TN23: Ashf 3D 34
Bryony Dr. TN23: Kgnt 4G 39
BUCKLAND 1B 28
Buckland Av. CT16: Dover 1B 28
Buckland Ct. CT16: Dover 6B 16
BUCKLAND HOSPITAL 2A 28
Buckland Mill CT17: Dover 1A 28
BUCKLAND VALLEY 6B 16
Bucksford La. TN23: Ashf 5B 34
Buckthorn Cl. CT14: Deal 4G 9
Buffs Av. CT20: F'stone 1B 58
Bulleid Pl. TN24: Ashf 6H 35
Bullrushes, The TN26: Shad 5C 38
  (off Bethersden Rd.)
Bulls Cotts. CT21: Hythe 6D 56
  (off St Leonard's Rd.)
Bulls Pas. CT21: Hythe 5E 57
  (off Dental St.)
Bull Yard, The TN24: Ashf 3B 4
Bulrushes, The TN23: Ashf 5A 34
Bulwark Rd. CT14: Deal 4H 9
Bulwark St. CT17: Dover 6D 28
Bungalows, The TN30: Tent 6D 64
Bunker's Hill CT17: Dover 1A 28
Bunkers Hill Av. CT17: Dover 2A 28
Bunkers Hill Rd. CT17: Dover 2A 28
Burgate Ter. TN25: Mers 3G 41
Burgess Cl. CT16: Whitf 2B 16
Burgess Grn. CT14: Hackl 3A 8
Burgess Row TN30: Tent 6A 64
Burgoyne Gro. CT16: Whitf 4A 16
Burgoyne Hgts. CT15: Gus 1E 29
Burleigh Ct. TN24: W'boro 3D 36
Burlington Ho. CT16: Dover 5F 7
BURMARSH 5A 62

Burmarsh Rd. CT21: Hythe 2E 63
  TN29: Burm, Dym 5A 62
Burrow Rd. CT17: F'stone 1D 60
Burton Cl. CT19: F'stone 6G 49
Burton Rd. TN24: Kenn 5A 32
Bushy Royds TN24: W'boro 1H 39
Bushy Ruff Cotts. CT16: Temp E 5F 15
Bushy Ruff Country Pk. 5E 15
Butt Fld. Rd. TN23: Ashf 5C 34
Butternut Copse TN23: Ashf 2B 34
Butterside Rd. TN23: Kgnt 3G 39
Butts, The CT4: Elham 1H 21
Buzzlines Stadium 1G 59
BYBROOK 6H 31
Bybrook Ct. TN24: Kenn 1G 35
Bybrook Fld. CT20: S'gte 4E 59
Bybrook Rd. TN24: Kenn 1H 35
Bybrook Way CT20: S'gte 3E 59
Byllan Rd. CT17: Dover 6G 15
Byron Cres. CT16: Dover 5B 16

C

Cade Rd. TN23: Ashf 6F 35
Cades Rd. TN26: Hoth 1D 30
Caesar Av. TN23: Kgnt 2D 38
Caesars Way CT19: F'stone 6E 49
Calgary Cres. CT19: F'stone 5C 50
Calgary Ter. CT16: Dover 6B 16
  (off Alberta Cl.)
Calland TN25: Sme 2D 42
Cambridge Gdns. CT20: F'stone 4F 5 (2B 60)
Cambridge Rd. CT14: Walm 2H 11
  CT17: Dover 6E 7 (5D 28)
Cambridge Ter. CT16: Dover 6F 7 (4E 29)
  CT20: F'stone 4H 5 (2C 60)
Camden Cres. CT16: Dover 6F 7 (4E 29)
Camden Ter. TN24: W'boro 4A 36
Cameron Ct. CT17: Dover 5A 28
Campbell Rd. CT14: Walm 1H 11
  CT18: H'nge .6G 23
Campbell Wlk. CT18: H'nge 6G 23
Canada Cl. CT19: F'stone 1C 58
Canada Rd. CT14: Walm 1G 11
Cannongate Av. CT21: Hythe 4F 57
Cannongate Cl. CT21: Hythe 5G 57
Cannongate Gdns. CT21: Hythe 4G 57
Cannongate Rd. CT21: Hythe 4F 57
Cannon St. CT14: Deal 4G 9
  CT16: Dover 4E 7 (4D 28)
Canons Ga. Rd. CT16: Dover 4G 7 (3E 29)
Canon Woods Way TN24: Kenn 5B 32
Canterbury Cl. CT19: F'stone 1H 5
Canterbury Ct. TN24: Ashf 3H 35
Canterbury Rd.
  CT4: Elham, O'nge . . . . .3E 21 & 3G 21
  CT15: Lyd'n .2A 14
  CT15: S'fld .3G 23
  CT18: D'sole, H'nge 3G 23
  CT18: Etch'l .1F 47
  CT18: F'stone, H'nge 1G 5 (4A 50)
  CT18: Lym'ge 3E 21
  CT19: F'stone 6B 50
  TN24: Ashf, Kenn 2G 4 (2G 35)
  (not continuous)
  TN24: W'boro 1A 40
  TN25: Bou A, Bou L, Kenn 1G 35
  TN25: Bra L, E Bra 2E 43
Canute Rd. CT14: Deal 2G 9
Canute Wlk. CT14: Deal 2G 9
Capel Cl. TN23: Ashf 4D 34
Capel Ct. Pk. CT18: Cap F 3G 51
CAPEL-LE-FERNE 3G 51
Capel St. CT15: Hou 6G 25
  CT18: Cap F .3F 51
Capstan Row CT14: Deal 5H 9
Captains Ct. CT21: Hythe 6E 57
Captain Webb Memorial 5G 7
Captain Webbs CT17: Dover 6A 6
Carlsden Cl. CT17: Dover 6A 16
Carlton Leas CT20: F'stone 6E 5 (3A 60)
Carlton Rd. CT14: Kgdn 1G 13
  TN23: Ashf .2E 35
Caroland Cl. TN25: Sme 2D 42
Caroland Vs. TN25: Sme 3D 42
Carter Cl. CT18: H'nge 6G 23
Carters Rd. CT20: F'stone 2F 59

Cassino Sq. CT15: Gus 1E 29
Castalia Cotts. CT14: Walm 2H 11
  (off Cambridge Rd.)
Castle Av. CT16: Dover 1D 6 (2D 28)
  CT21: Hythe .4D 56
Castle Bay CT14: S'gte 4C 58
Castle Cl. CT20: S'gte 4F 59
  CT21: Lymp .5D 54
Castle Cotts. TN25: Westw 3D 30
Castle Cres. CT21: Salt 3E 57
Castle Dr. CT16: Whitf 3H 15
Castle Hill CT19: F'stone 4F 5
Castle Hill Av. CT16: Dover 6E 5 (2A 60)
Castle Hill Rd. CT16: Dover 2G 7 (2E 29)
Castle Ho. CT20: F'stone 6E 5
Castle M. CT14: Deal 2F 11
Castlemount Ct. CT16: Dover 3F 7 (3E 29)
Castlemount Rd. CT16: Dover 2E 7 (2D 28)
Castle Rd. CT20: S'gte 4F 59
  CT21: Hythe, Salt 3D 56
Castle St. CT16: Dover 5E 7 (4D 28)
  TN23: Ashf 3B 4 (3F 35)
Castleton Retail Cen.
  CT16: Dover 2C 6 (2C 28)
Castleview Cl. CT17: Dover 1A 6 (2B 28)
Castle Wlk. CT14: Deal 2H 9
Cauldham Cl. CT18: Cap F 4F 51
Cauldham La. CT18: Cap F 3F 51
Cavalry Ct. CT14: Walm 2H 11
Cavell Sq. CT14: Deal 2E 11
Cavenagh Rd. CT15: St Marg 3F 19
Caves Ct. CT16: Dover 4E 7
Caxton Cl. TN30: Tent 6A 64
Caxton Ho. TN24: Ashf 2D 4 (2G 35)
Cecil Ct. TN24: Ashf 2B 4 (2F 35)
Cecil Rd. CT14: Walm 6H 11
Cedar Cl. TN23: Ashf 2C 34
  CT20: F'stone 2E 59
  TN30: Tent .6A 64
Cedars, The TN25: S'ndge 5B 44
Cedar Ter. CT16: Dover 6C 16
  (off Selkirk Rd.)
  TN25: S'ndge 5B 44
Celtic Rd. CT14: Deal 2E 11
Cemetery Cotts. CT18: H'nge 1F 49
Cemetery La. TN24: Kenn 1G 35
Central Service Rd. CT16: Dover 3H 29
Centre Rd. CT17: Dover 5C 28
Centurion Pk. CT19: F'stone 6E 49
Centurion Wlk. TN23: Kgnt 3F 39
Century Wlk. CT14: Deal 5G 9
Chaffinch Dr. TN23: Kgnt 4G 39
Chaffinch Lodge CT16: Dover 1B 28
Chalcroft Rd. CT20: F'stone 3E 59
Chalk Av. TN30: St Mic 3B 64
Chalk Cl. CT19: F'stone 6G 49
Chalk Hill Rd. CT14: Kgdn 2G 13
Chalksole Grn. La. CT15: Alk 1E 25
Chalkwell Ct. CT17: Dover 4A 28
Chamberlain Rd. CT17: Dover 3A 28
Chance Mdw. CT15: Gus 3F 17
Channel Cl. CT19: F'stone 6D 50
Channel Ho. CT20: F'stone 3G 5
Channel Lea CT14: Walm 4G 11
Channel Tunnel Rail Terminal 5B 48
Channel Vw. CT19: F'stone 4H 5
Channel Vw. Rd. CT17: Dover 5C 28
Chapel Cl. CT18: Etch'l 2F 47
Chapel La. CT4: R Min 1C 20
  CT14: Ripp .5A 10
  CT15: St Marg 3D 18
  CT16: Dover .5E 7
Chapel M. TN24: Ashf 3C 4
Chapel Pl. CT17: Dover 5E 7 (4D 28)
Chapel Rd. CT16: Whitf 1A 16
Chapel Row TN23: Kgnt 4E 39
Chapel St. CT14: Deal 5H 9
  CT21: Hythe .5D 56
Chapman Ho. CT14: Deal 2F 11
Charles Cres. CT19: F'stone 6E 49
Charles Ho. CT14: Deal 2F 11
  (off Brambles Ct. Yd.)
Charles Lister Ct. CT17: Dover 1A 6 (2B 28)
Charles Rd. CT14: Deal 2E 11
Charles St. CT14: Deal 1F 11
Charlotte St. CT20: F'stone 3H 5 (2C 60)
Charlton Av. CT16: Dover 1C 6 (2C 28)
Charlton Cen. CT16: Dover 3C 6 (2C 28)
Charlton Cl. TN24: W'boro 5C 36

Charlton Grn.—Coolinge Rd.

Charlton Grn. CT16: Dover 1C 6 (2C 28)
Charlton Ho. CT16: Dover 3D 6
Charminster TN23: Ashf 1C 38
Chart Av. TN23: Ashf, Gt Cha 4A 34
Chart Ent. Pk. TN23: Ashf 4E 35
Charter Ho. CT16: Dover 6F 7
TN24: Ashf 3C 4 (3G 35)
Chart Leacon Cotts. TN23: Gt Cha 3C 34
Chart Rd. CT19: F'stone 1F 59
TN23: Ashf 6A 34
(not continuous)
TN23: Ashf, Gt Cha 2A 4 (4A 34)
TN24: Ashf 2A 4 (2E 35)
Chart Rd. Ind. Est. TN23: Ashf 2E 35
Chartwell Rd. TN25: Mers 5H 39
Chase, The CT15: St Marg 1D 18
Chater Cl. TN23: Ashf 5A 34
Chater Ct. CT14: Deal 1G 11
Chaucer Cres. CT16: Dover 6B 16
Cheddar Cl. TN24: Ashf 1A 4 (1F 35)
CHEESEMAN'S GREEN 5B 40
Cheeseman's Grn. La.
TN24: Svgtn 5B 40
TN25: Mers 6H 39
(not continuous)
Chelsea Ct. CT21: Hythe 6E 57
Chequers Pk. TN25: Wye 2G 33
CHERITON 1E 59
Cheriton Ct. Rd. CT20: F'stone 1C 58
Cheriton Gdns. CT20: F'stone 4E 5 (2A 60)
Cheriton High St. CT18: F'stone 1B 58
CT19: F'stone 1D 58
CHERITON HILL 4D 48
Cheriton Pl. CT14: Walm 1H 11
CT20: F'stone 5F 5 (3B 60)
Cheriton Rd. CT14: Walm 1H 11
CT19: F'stone 1F 59
CT20: F'stone 4E 5 (2A 60)
Cheriton Wood Ho. CT19: F'stone 6D 48
Cherry Brook Rd. CT20: F'stone 1E 59
Cherry Ct. CT19: F'stone 1G 59
Cherry Gdn. Av. CT19: F'stone 1G 59
Cherry Gdn. Cres. TN25: Wye 1H 33
Cherry Gdn. La. CT19: F'stone 6F 49
TN25: Wye 1H 33
Cherry Gdns. CT4: Elham 1H 21
TN23: Ashf 2E 39
Cherry Glebe TN25: Mers 4G 41
Cherry La. CT14: Gt Mon 2B 10
Cherry Orchard TN30: Tent 6A 64
Cherry Tree Av. CT16: Dover 1B 6 (2C 28)
Cherrywood Ri. TN25: Ashf 1D 34
Chestnut Cl. CT16: Whitf 1A 16
CT21: Hythe 6A 56
TN23: Ashf 2C 34
TN30: Tent 4C 64
Chestnut La. TN23: Kgnt 3G 39
Chestnut Rd. CT17: Dover 4B 28
Chestnuts, The TN25: Sme 2D 42
TN25: S'ndge 4B 44
Chestnut Ter. CT21: Hythe 6C 56
Chevalier Rd. CT17: Dover 4A 28
Cheviot Way TN24: Ashf 1G 35
Chichester Cl. TN23: Ashf 6A 4 (4F 35)
Chichester Rd. CT20: S'gte 3E 59
Chilham Ho. TN23: Ashf 1D 38
Chilham Rd. CT19: F'stone 1E 59
Chilmington Caravan Pk. TN23: Gt Cha 1A 38
CHILMINGTON GREEN 2A 38
Chilmington Grn. La.
TN23: Gt Cha . . . . .2A 38 & 3A 38
Chiltern End TN24: Ashf 1A 4 (2F 35)
Chilton Av. CT16: Temp E 5E 15
Chilton Ct. CT20: F'stone 2H 5 (1C 60)
Chilton Way CT17: Dover 6F 15
Chimes, The TN24: Ashf 1C 4 (2G 35)
Chislet Ho. *TN23: Ashf* *1D 38*
(off Frinsted Gdns.)
Chislett Cl. TN25: S'ndge 3C 44
Chisnall Rd. CT17: Dover 5G 15
Christchurch Ct. CT17: Dover 5D 6 (4D 28)
Christ Chu. Rd. CT20: F'stone 5E 5 (2A 60)
Christchurch Rd. TN23: Ashf 6A 4 (4F 35)
Christchurch Way CT16: Dover 6B 16
Christopher Bushell Way TN24: Kenn 1A 36
Chunnel Ind. Est. TN23: Ashf 6B 4 (4F 35)
Church Cliff CT14: Kgdn 1H 13
Church Cl. TN25: Mers 4G 41
Church Cotts. TN30: St Mic 2A 64
Church Ct. CT18: Lym'ge 5E 21
Church Fld. TN25: Stanf 4F 45
Churchfield Way TN25: Wye 1F 33
Church Grn. Cotts. TN25: Sme 3C 42
Church Haven CT14: R'wld 2D 12
Church Hill CT16: Temp E 4F 15
CT18: H'nge 2B 50
CT21: Hythe 5E 57
TN23: Kgnt 4E 39
CHURCH HOUGHAM 1D 52
Church Ho. CT14: Deal 4G 9
Churchill Av. CT14: Walm 3G 11
CT19: F'stone 5G 49
Churchill Cl. CT15: St Marg 4D 18
CT19: F'stone 5B 50
Churchill Ct. *CT17: Dover* *1B 28*
(off London Rd.)
CT21: Hythe 6D 56
Churchill Ho. *CT20: F'stone* *2F 59*
(off Coolinge La.)
Churchill Ho. Hgts. *CT16: Dover* *6B 16*
(off Hudson Cl.)
Churchill Rd. CT17: Dover 5A 28
Churchill St. CT16: Dover 2C 6 (2C 28)
Churchill Wlk. CT18: H'nge 1F 49
Church La. CT14: Deal 6D 8
CT14: Ripp 5B 10
CT14: R'wld 2D 12
CT15: Chu H 6D 26
CT15: E Lan 1G 17
CT15: Lyd'n 2A 14
TN23: Kgnt 4F 39
TN25: Aldtn, S'ndge 6E 43
TN25: M Hor 1D 44
TN26: Hoth 2C 30
TN26: Shad 6C 38
Church Mdws. CT14: Deal 5E 9
Church Path CT14: Deal 1E 11
(not continuous)
CT14: Gt Mon 2B 10
CT14: Walm 4G 11
TN30: Tent 6A 64
Church Ri. CT21: Hythe 5D 56
Church Rd. CT17: Dover 4A 28
CT18: Lym'ge 4E 21
CT20: F'stone 1C 58
CT21: Hythe 5E 57
TN23: Ashf 5C 4 (4G 35)
TN24: Kenn 5A 32
TN24: Svgtn 6C 36
(not continuous)
TN24: W'boro 5B 36
TN25: Mers 4F 41
TN25: Sme 3C 42
TN29: Burm 4A 62
TN30: Tent 6A 64
Church St. CT14: Walm 4F 11
CT16: Dover 4E 7 (4D 28)
CT20: F'stone 5G 5 (3B 60)
TN25: Wye 1G 33
Church Wlk. *CT4: Elham* *2H 21*
(off Pound La.)
CHURCH WHITFIELD 1C 16
Church Whitfield Rd. CT15: Whitf 1B 16
CT16: Whitf 1B 16
Church Yd. TN23: Ashf 4B 4 (3F 35)
Church Yd. Pas. TN23: Ashf 4B 4
Cineworld Cinema
Ashford 6G 31
Cinque Ports Av. CT21: Hythe 6D 56
Circular Rd. CT16: Dover 2H 29
(not continuous)
Citadel Cres. CT17: Dover 5B 28
Citadel Hgts. CT17: Dover 5B 28
Citadel Rd. CT17: Dover 5B 28
Clanwilliam Rd. CT14: Deal 6H 9
Claremont Cl. CT14: Kgdn 1G 13
Claremont Rd. CT14: Deal 6F 9
CT14: Kgdn 1G 13
CT20: F'stone 4E 5 (2A 60)
Clarence Pl. CT14: Deal 4H 9
CT17: Dover 6D 28
Clarence Rd. CT14: Walm 2H 11
CT18: Cap F 4F 51
Clarence St. CT20: F'stone 3G 5 (2B 60)
CLARENDON 6A 6 (4B 28)
Clarendon Pl. CT17: Dover 6A 6 (4B 28)
Clarendon Rd. CT17: Dover 6C 6 (4C 28)
Clarendon St. CT17: Dover 6A 6 (4B 28)
Claridge M. *CT21: Hythe* *5E 57*
(off Chapel St.)
Clarke Cres. TN24: Kenn 6A 32
Clarkes Cl. CT14: Deal 1D 10
Claudius Gro. TN23: Kgnt 2D 38
Claygate TN23: Ashf 2C 38
Cleveland Cl. CT16: Dover 6B 16
Cleves Way TN23: Ashf 5C 34
Cliff Cl. CT21: Hythe 4F 57
Cliffe Ho. CT20: F'stone 4G 59
Cliffe Path CT15: St Marg 6C 18
Cliffe Rd. CT14: Kgdn 1H 13
Clifford Gdns. CT14: Deal 3F 11
Clifford Pk. CT14: Walm 5F 11
Cliff Rd. CT20: F'stone 4G 59
CT21: Hythe 4F 57
Cliffstone Ct. CT20: F'stone 2H 59
Clifton Cres. CT20: F'stone 4H 59
Clifton Gdns. CT20: F'stone 6E 5 (3A 60)
Clifton Mans. CT20: F'stone 3A 60
Clifton Rd. CT20: F'stone 3A 60
Clim Down CT14: Kgdn 1H 13
Clive Dennis Ct. TN24: W'boro 4A 36
Clockhouse TN23: Ashf 4C 34
Close, The CT15: Lyd'n 1B 14
CT19: F'stone *5C 50*
(off Fleming Way)
CT21: Salt 3D 56
TN23: Ashf 6D 34
TN25: Wye 1G 33
Clouston Cl. CT18: H'nge 6H 23
Clover Ct. TN24: W'boro 1H 39
Clynton Way TN23: Ashf 6E 35
Coach Dr. TN26: Hoth 1D 30
Coach Rd. CT18: Acr, D'sole 3E 23
Coastguard Cotts. CT14: Kgdn 3H 13
CT16: Dover 3G 29
CT21: Hythe 6D 56
Cobay Cl. CT21: Hythe 5F 57
Cobbs M. CT20: F'stone 5E 5 (3A 60)
Cobbs Pas. CT21: Hythe 5E 57
Cobbswood Ind. Est. TN23: Ashf 3D 34
Cobden Rd. CT19: F'stone 1E 59
CT21: Hythe 6D 56
Cobham Ho. CT16: Dover 3E 7
Cobs, The TN30: Tent 6A 64
Cock La. CT4: Elham 2H 21
Coldblow CT14: Walm 6D 10
Coldharbour La. TN25: Wye 1H 33
Coldred Hill CT15: Cold, Lyd'n 1B 14
Colemans Cl. TN23: Kgnt 2B 38
Colin's Way CT21: Hythe 4A 58
Collard Pl. CT18: H'nge 6G 23
Collard Rd. TN24: W'boro 6C 36
Collards La. CT4: Elham 3G 21
College Ct. TN23: Ashf 4C 4 (3G 35)
College Rd. CT14: Deal 3H 9
College Row *CT17: Dover* *4B 28*
(off Elms Va. Rd.)
Collie Dr. TN23: Kgnt 2C 38
Collingbourne TN23: Ashf 1C 38
Collingwood Ct. *CT20: F'stone* *2E 59*
(off Collingwood Ri.)
Collingwood Ri. CT20: F'stone 2E 59
Collingwood Rd. CT15: St Marg 2C 18
Collingwood Rd. E. CT15: St Marg 6E 13
Collison Pl. TN30: Tent 6D 64
Colonel Stephens Railway Mus. 5A 64
Colonel Stephens Way TN30: Tent 4A 64
Colorado Cl. CT16: Dover 6B 16
Colton Cres. CT16: Dover 5B 16
Common La. CT17: Dover 6G 15
Common Way TN26: Hoth 1D 30
Concept Ct. CT19: F'stone 6F 49
Conifers, The CT14: Walm 3E 11
Coniston Rd. CT19: F'stone 1H 59
Conker Cl. TN23: Kgnt 4G 39
Connaught Rd. CT16: Dover 1D 6 (2D 28)
CT20: F'stone 4F 5 (2B 60)
Connect 10 TN24: Svgtn 1C 40
Conrad Ho. CT17: Dover 4A 6 (3B 28)
Constables Rd. CT16: Dover 2G 7 (2E 29)
Constancia Ct. CT20: F'stone 4E 5
Constantine Rd. TN23: Kgnt 2D 38
Convent Cl. CT15: St Marg 3E 19
Conway Cl. CT21: Salt 3D 56
COOLINGE 3F 59
Coolinge La. CT20: F'stone 2F 59
Coolinge Rd. CT20: F'stone 4E 5 (2A 60)

A-Z Ashford 69

Coombe Cl. CT17: Dover 2A 28
Coombe Cl. CT17: Dover 2A 28
Coombe La. TN30: Tent 6A 64
Coombe Rd. CT15: Dover, Hou 4D 26
  CT17: Dover .4D 26
  CT19: F'stone .1F 59
Coombe Valley Rd. CT17: Dover . . .1A 6 (3A 28)
Coombe Way CT18: H'nge 1A 50
Coombe Wood La. CT18: H'nge 1H 49
Coopers Cl. TN25: Bra L 1D 42
Cooper's La. TN25: S'ndge 5F 43
Copperfield Cl. TN24: Kenn 5G 31
Copperwood TN24: Ashf 1D 4 (1G 35)
Coppin St. CT14: Deal 5H 9
Copse, The TN23: Ashf 2B 34
Copthall Gdns. CT20: F'stone 4F 5 (2B 60)
Corbett Rd. CT18: H'nge 2F 49
Cordova Ct. CT20: F'stone 3H 59
Cornbrook Rd. CT21: Hythe 1H 63
Corner Fld. TN23: Kgnt 2F 39
Corner Ho. Bldgs. CT21: Hythe 5D 56
  (off Canterbury Rd.)
Cornes Cl. TN24: W'boro 4C 36
Corniche, The CT20: S'gte 4C 58
Cornwall Ho. CT14: Deal 6E 9
  CT17: Dover 5D 6
Cornwallis Av. CT19: F'stone 1H 59
Cornwallis Cl. CT19: F'stone 1H 59
  TN24: W'boro .6D 36
Cornwall Rd. CT14: Walm 2G 11
Coronation Cotts. CT19: F'stone 1D 58
  (off Cheriton High St.)
Coronation Dr. TN23: Gt Cha 4A 34
Coronation Pde. CT19: F'stone 2D 60
Corone Cl. CT19: F'stone 6G 49
Corunna Cl. CT21: Hythe 5C 56
Corunna Pl. CT15: Gus 6E 17
Cotswold Cl. TN24: Ashf 1B 4 (1F 35)
Coulter Rd. TN23: Ashf, Kgnt 1B 38
Country Way TN23: Kgnt 3F 39
  (off Roman Way)
County Sq. Shop. Cen. TN23: Ashf . .4B 4 (3F 35)
Court App. CT20: F'stone 3A 60
Courtenay Rd. CT14: Deal 3G 9
Court Hill Ho. CT16: Dover 5G 15
Courtland Av. CT16: Whitf 3A 16
Courtland Dr. CT16: Dover 5G 15
Courtlands CT14: Kgdn 1H 13
Court Lodge CT14: Deal 5F 9
  (off Church La.)
Court Lodge Cotts. TN25: Hin 3F 37
Court Pl. CT20: F'stone 3A 60
Court Rd. CT14: Walm 4E 11
Courtside Sports Facility 1D 38
Court Wurtin TN23: Ashf 6E 35
Courtyard, The CT14: Deal 2F 11
  TN24: Ashf 1B 40
Coventry Ct. CT14: Deal 1G 11
  (off Coventry Gdns.)
Coventry Gdns. CT14: Walm 1G 11
Covert TN23: Ashf 4C 34
Cowdray Rd. CT14: Deal 2E 11
Cowdray Sq. CT14: Deal 2F 11
Cowdrey Cl. TN24: W'boro 6C 36
Cowgate Hill CT17: Dover 5E 7 (4D 28)
Cowgate La. CT18: H'nge 5A 24
Cow La. CT17: Dover 4A 28
Cowper Rd. CT14: Deal 6F 9
  CT17: Dover 1G 27
Cox Dr. CT18: H'nge 6G 23
Coxhill Cres. CT17: Dover 6F 15
Coxhill Gdns. CT17: Dover 6F 15
CRABBLE 6H 15
Crabble Athletic Ground 1H 27
Crabble Av. CT17: Dover 1A 28
Crabble Cl. CT17: Dover 1H 27
Crabble Corn Mill 6H 15
Crabble Hgts. CT17: Dover 6H 15
Crabble Hill CT17: Dover 6A 16
Crabble La. CT17: Dover 2G 27
Crabble Mdws. CT17: Dover 1A 28
Crabble Rd. CT17: Dover 6A 16
Cradle Bri. Dr. TN24: W'boro 3A 36
Crafford St. CT16: Dover 3D 6 (2D 28)
Cramp App. CT16: Dover 3G 29
Cranbrooks TN25: Mers 4E 41
Cranleigh Dr. CT16: Whitf 2A 16
Cranswick Cotts. CT14: Ripp 5A 10

Craufurd Grn. CT20: F'stone 2D 58
Craythorne TN30: Tent 5B 64
Craythorne Cl. CT21: Hythe 3B 58
Crescent, The CT15: St Marg 4E 19
  CT20: S'gte 4E 59
  TN24: Ashf 1B 40
Cressfield TN23: Ashf 4D 34
Crete Rd. E. CT18: F'stone 4A 50
Crete Rd. W. CT18: F'stone 4D 48
Creteway Cl. CT19: F'stone 5C 50
Cricketers Cl. CT18: H'nge 5H 23
Crimond Av. TN29: Dym 5E 63
Criol La. TN26: Shad 4A 38
Cripps La. CT15: St Marg 3D 18
Croft, The TN30: Tent 6B 64
Crofters Cl. CT21: Hythe 6A 56
Crofton Cl. TN24: Kenn 5G 31
Croft Rd. CT18: Ashf 3H 35
Croft Rd. Flats TN24: Ashf 3H 35
  (off Croft Rd.)
Croftwood TN23: Ashf 1B 38
Crombie Cl. CT18: H'nge 6H 23
Cromwell Pk. Pl. CT20: F'stone 3D 58
Crooked's Rd. CT14: Ripp 6C 10
Crook's Ct. La. CT15: W Hou 1B 52
Cross Rd. CT14: Deal, Walm 4E 11
  CT15: St Marg .5D 18
Cross Stile TN23: Ashf 5D 34
Crothall Haven TN24: Ashf 2B 4
Crowbridge Link TN24: W'boro 1B 40
Crowbridge Rd. TN24: Ashf 6A 36
Crown Ct. CT14: Deal 5H 9
  (off Middle St.)
Crownfield Rd. TN23: Ashf 5G 35
Crundale Cl. CT18: Ashf 1D 38
Cruttenden Cl. TN30: Tent 6C 64
Cryol Rd. TN23: Ashf 6D 34
C S Rolls Statue .5F 7
Cubitt Ho. CT19: F'stone 2G 5
Cuckoo La. CT21: Post 3B 46
  TN23: Ashf 1B 38
  (Coulter Rd.)
  TN23: Ashf 1C 38
  (Summerhill)
Cudworth Rd. TN24: W'boro 6A 36
Cullens Hill CT4: Elham 2G 21
Culling's Hill CT4: Elham 2H 21
Culter Fld. TN23: Ashf 5C 34
Curlew Pl. CT18: H'nge 2G 49
Curteis Rd. TN30: Tent 4B 64
Curtis Rd. TN24: W'boro 6A 36
Curzon Cl. CT14: Walm 2G 11
Curzon Rd. CT17: Dover 4A 6 (3B 28)
Cygnet Way TN23: Ashf 4D 34
Cylinder Rd. CT21: Salt 3D 56
Cypress Av. TN23: Ashf 3C 34

D

Dairy M. CT14: Gt Mon 1C 10
Dale Wlk. TN24: Kenn 4G 31
Dallas Brett Cres. CT19: F'stone 5C 50
Dalmatia Ct. CT17: Dover 2H 27
Dalmeny Ter. CT21: Hythe 5C 56
  (off Dymchurch Rd.)
Damara Way TN25: Mers 5H 39
Danemore TN30: Tent 5B 64
Danes Ct. CT16: Dover 1D 28
  (not continuous)
Dane Vs. CT18: H'nge 4E 49
Daniels Pl. CT18: H'nge 6A 24
Danton La. CT18: F'stone 4C 48
Darby Pl. CT20: F'stone 3F 5 (2B 60)
Darby Rd. CT20: F'stone 3F 5 (2B 60)
Dark La. CT21: Hythe 4C 56
Darlinghurst Rd. CT19: F'stone 6E 49
Darlington St. CT20: F'stone 3F 5 (2B 60)
Darnley Cl. CT17: Dover 3F 59
Darracott Cl. CT14: Deal 6F 9
David Henderson Av. TN23: Ashf 2C 34
Davis Av. CT14: Deal 1E 11
Dawbourne TN30: St Mic 2B 64
Dawson Rd. CT19: F'stone 1G 5 (1B 60)
DEAL 5H 9
Deal Castle 6H 9
Deal Castle Rd. CT14: Deal 6H 9
Deal Indoor Tennis Cen. 1G 11

Deal Maritime & Local History Mus. 5H 9
Deal Pier 5H 9
Deal Rd. CT14: N'bne 2A 10
  CT15: Dover, Gus 2E 29
  CT16: Dover 1G 7 (2E 29)
Deal Station (Rail) 5G 9
Dean Mead CT19: F'stone 6H 49
Dean's Wlk. TN23: Ashf 6D 34
Deanwood Rd. CT17: Dover 2G 27
De Bradelei Wharf CT17: Dover . . .6E 7 (4D 28)
De Burgh St. CT17: Dover 3C 6 (3C 28)
Deedes Cl. CT21: Hythe 4E 57
Defiant Cl. CT18: H'nge 2G 49
De Havilland Cl. CT18: H'nge 2H 49
Delane Rd. CT14: Deal 6E 9
Demozay Cl. CT18: H'nge 1G 49
Denbigh Pl. TN23: Ashf 5F 35
Dencora Way TN23: Ashf 4E 35
Dene, The CT21: Hythe 5E 57
Denham Cl. TN29: Dym 5F 63
Denmark St. CT19: F'stone 1H 5 (1C 60)
Denmark Ter. TN23: Ashf 5G 35
Dennes Mill Cl. TN25: Wye 1F 33
Denness Rd. TN23: Ashf 6F 35
Dennis Way CT19: F'stone 6E 49
DENSOLE 3G 23
Densole La. CT18: D'sole 3G 23
Densole Way CT18: D'sole 3G 23
Dental St. CT21: Hythe 5E 57
Dering Rd. TN24: Ashf 3H 35
Devon Av. CT14: Walm 1G 11
Devon Rd. CT19: F'stone 3F 5 (2B 60)
Devonshire Rd. CT17: Dover 4A 6 (3B 28)
Dexter Cl. TN25: Kenn 3G 31
Deyley Way TN23: Ashf 5A 34
Diamond Cl. CT19: F'stone 6F 49
Diana Gdns. CT14: Deal 6E 9
Dibdin Rd. CT14: Deal 4H 9
Dickson Rd. CT17: Dover 3B 6 (3C 28)
Dieu Stone La. CT16: Dover 4E 7 (3D 28)
Digby Rd. CT20: F'stone 2E 59
Dixwell Rd. CT20: F'stone 3G 59
Dock Exit Rd. CT16: Dover 3F 29
Doctor's La. CT15: Chu H 1D 52
Dodds La. CT16: Dover 6A 16
Dog Kennel La. CT18: Lym'ge 4D 20
Dola Av. CT14: Deal 5F 9
  (not continuous)
Dolphin Ct. CT21: Hythe 6E 57
  (off Whitegate Cl.)
Dolphin Ho. CT16: Dover 5F 7
Dolphin La. CT16: Dover 5F 7 (4E 29)
Dolphin Pas. CT16: Dover 5F 7 (4E 29)
Dolphin Rd. CT16: Dover 5F 7 (4E 29)
Dolphins Rd. CT19: F'stone 1F 5 (6A 50)
Dolphin St. CT14: Deal 4H 9
DONKEY STREET 4B 62
Donkey St. TN29: Burm 5A 62
Dorset Ct. CT14: Walm 3H 11
Dorset Gdns. CT14: Walm 3G 11
Dossett Cl. CT14: Deal 3E 11
Douglas Av. CT21: Hythe 5E 57
Douglas Cl. CT14: Deal 2E 11
  CT17: Dover 3A 6 (3B 28)
Douglas Ter. CT14: Deal 4H 9
Dour House, The CT16: Dover 3E 7 (3D 28)
Dour M. CT16: Dover 1C 6
Douro Pl. CT16: Dover 5G 7 (4E 29)
Dour Side CT17: Dover 6H 15
Dour St. CT16: Dover 3D 6 (3D 28)
Dour Ter. CT16: Temp E 4F 15
Dove Cl. CT21: Hythe 1H 63
  TN23: Kgnt 4G 39
Dovedale Cl. TN24: Ashf 1A 4 (2E 35)
Dove Lea Gdns. CT17: Dover 6G 15
DOVER 3D 6 (3D 28)
Dover Athletic FC 1H 27
Dover Bus. Pk. CT16: Whitf 3B 16
Dover Castle 3H 7 (3F 29)
DOVER COMMUNITY HOSPITAL 3E 7
  (off Maison Dieu)
Dover Discovery Cen. 5E 7 (4D 28)
DOVER HILL 5D 50
Dover Hill CT19: F'stone 5C 50
Dover Leisure Cen. 4G 7 (3E 29)
Dover Museum & Bronze Age Boat Gallery
  . . . . .5E 7
Dover Patrol Memorial 2G 19

Dover Pl. TN23: Ashf 5C **4** (4G **35**)
Dover Priory Station (Rail) 5C **6** (3C **28**)
Dover Rd. CT14: R'wld, Walm 3D **12**
  CT15: Gus .6E **17**
  CT15: St Marg 4H **17**
  CT18: Cap F .3G **51**
  CT19: F'stone 2H **5** (6C **50**)
  CT20: F'stone 3G **5** (2B **60**)
Dover Sea Sports Cen. 6F **7** (5E **29**)
Dover Trade Cen. CT16: Whitf 3C **16**
Dover Transport Mus. 4A **16**
Dover Western Heights Viewpoint
. . . . .6C **6** (4C **28**)
Dowell M. CT14: Walm 2G **11**
Down Ct. TN23: Ashf 2C **38**
Downhill Cl. CT16: Temp E 3F **15**
Downland Ct. TN24: Ashf 2A **4** (2F **35**)
Downlands CT14: Walm 5F **11**
Downsberry Rd. TN25: Mers 5H **39**
Downs Cl. CT18: H'nge 1G **49**
Downside CT15: St Marg 3E **19**
  CT19: F'stone 6A **50**
Downside Rd. CT16: Whitf 2B **16**
Downs Rd. CT14: Walm 3F **11**
  CT19: F'stone 1F **5** (5A **50**)
Downs Way TN25: S'ndge 4A **44**
Dragonfly Cl. TN23: Ashf 5B **34**
Dragonfly Way CT18: H'nge 2H **49**
Drake Rd. TN24: W'boro 6C **36**
DRELLINGORE 4E **25**
Drew La. CT14: Deal 1G **11**
Drive, The CT14: Deal 6G **9**
Drop Redoubt Rd. CT17: Dover 6C **6** (5C **28**)
Drove, The CT16: Whitf 1A **16**
Drovers Rdbt. TN24: Ashf 1E **35**
Droveway, The CT15: St Marg 3E **19**
Droveway Gdns. CT15: St Marg 3E **19**
Drum La. TN23: Ashf 3B **4** (3F **35**)
Drum Major Dr. CT14: Deal 2F **11**
Drummond Gro. TN24: Ashf 5H **35**
Drury Rd. TN30: Tent 5A **64**
Dryden Rd. CT16: Dover 6B **16**
Duck La. TN26: Shad 6C **38**
Duck St. CT4: Elham 2H **21**
Duckworth Cl. TN24: W'boro 6C **36**
Dudley Rd. CT19: F'stone 2C **60**
  TN24: Kenn 6A **32**
Duke St. CT14: Deal 4H **9**
Dunedin Dr. CT16: Dover 6B **16**
Dunkery Ri. TN24: Ashf 1F **35**
Dunkirk Sq. CT15: Gus 6F **17**
Dunnett Rd. CT19: F'stone 1E **59**
Dunnock Rd. TN25: Kenn 4F **31**
Dunstan Ho. CT14: Deal 3G **9**
Durban Cres. CT16: Dover 5C **16**
Durham Cl. CT17: Dover 5D **6** (4D **28**)
Durham Hill CT17: Dover 5D **6** (4D **28**)
Durlocks, The CT19: F'stone 4H **5** (2C **60**)
Dyke Rd. CT19: F'stone 3H **5** (2C **60**)
Dymchurch Rd. CT21: Hythe . . . . .4F **63** & 6B **56**

E

Ealham Cl. TN24: W'boro 5C **36**
Earls Av. CT20: F'stone 3H **59**
  TN24: W'boro 4B **36**
Earlsfield Rd. CT21: Hythe 5F **57**
Earlsworth Ct. TN24: W'boro 1A **40**
Earlsworth Rd. TN24: W'boro 1H **39**
Eastbridge Ct. CT21: Hythe 4F **57**
                  (off Station Rd.)
Eastbrook Pl. CT16: Dover 4F **7** (3F **29**)
East Cliff CT16: Dover 4H **7** (3F **29**)
  CT19: F'stone 2C **60**
East Cliff & Warren Country Pk. 6E **51**
E. Cliff Gdns. CT19: F'stone 2C **60**
E. Cliff Pas. CT19: F'stone 2C **60**
E. Cliff Vs. CT19: F'stone 3H **5**
East Cross TN30: Tent 6B **64**
Eastern Av. TN23: Ashf 3A **4** (3G **35**)
Eastern Docks CT16: Dover 4G **29**
Eastern Gdns. CT16: Dover 5A **36**
Eastern Service Rd. CT16: Dover 3H **29**
Eastfields CT19: F'stone 2G **5** (1B **60**)
Eastfleet Caravan Pk. TN29: Dym 5E **63**
Eastgate Rd. TN30: Tent 4C **64**
East Hill TN24: Ashf 3D **4** (3G **35**)
  TN30: Tent .5B **64**

E. Kent Hunt Cotts. CT4: Elham 2G **21**
EAST LANGDON 1G **17**
E. Langdon Rd. CT15: E Lan 1G **17**
                 (not continuous)
  CT15: Gus .3E **17**
  CT15: Mart, Mart M 6A **12**
Eastmead Av. TN23: Ashf 5G **35**
Eastmead Trad. Est. TN23: Ashf 5G **35**
E. Mountain La. TN25: Kenn 4B **32**
E. Mountain La. Cotts. TN25: Kenn 5C **32**
E. Norman Rd. CT16: Dover 2G **7** (2E **29**)
East Ramp CT16: Dover 3G **29**
East Rd. CT20: F'stone 3D **58**
Eastry Cl. TN23: Ashf 1E **39**
E. Stour Ct. TN24: Ashf 4H **35**
E. Stour Way TN24: W'boro 1H **39**
East St. CT17: Dover 3B **6** (3C **28**)
  CT19: F'stone 2C **60**
  CT21: Hythe 5F **57**
  TN23: Ashf 4A **4** (3F **35**)
E. Weald Dr. TN30: Tent 4B **64**
East Well TN30: Tent 6A **64**
Eastwell Barn M. TN30: Tent 5A **64**
Eastwell Cl. TN26: Shad 5D **38**
Eastwell Grange TN25: Ashf 3G **31**
Eastwell Mdws. TN30: Tent 5A **64**
EASTWELL PARK 1H **31**
Eaton Rd. CT17: Dover 4B **28**
Eaves Rd. CT17: Dover 4A **28**
Eckford Cl. CT18: H'nge 1F **49**
Eclipse Bus. Pk. TN23: Ashf 3D **34**
Edgar Rd. CT14: Deal 2F **11**
  CT17: Dover 1A **6** (2B **28**)
Edge Hill Cl. CT20: F'stone 3D **58**
Edinburgh Ho. CT14: Deal 6E **9**
  CT17: Dover 5D **6**
Edinburgh Pl. CT20: F'stone 4H **59**
                 (off Earls Av.)
Edinburgh Rd. TN24: Ashf 3B **4** (3F **35**)
Edmonton Ho. CT16: Dover 6B **16**
                 (off Alberta Cl.)
Edred Rd. CT17: Dover 3A **6** (3B **28**)
Edward Rd. CT14: Kgdn 1G **13**
  CT19: F'stone 1F **5** (1B **60**)
Edwards Rd. CT16: Dover 4D **6** (3D **28**)
Edward Ter. CT20: F'stone 1C **60**
                 (off Folly Rd.)
Effingham Cres. CT17: Dover 4D **6** (3D **28**)
Effingham Pas. CT17: Dover 5D **6** (4D **28**)
Effingham St. CT17: Dover 4D **6** (3D **28**)
Egerton Rd. CT16: Dover 5G **15**
Egerton Vs. CT19: F'stone 6C **50**
Eggringe TN23: Ashf 4C **34**
Eight Acres CT15: W Hou 5H **25**
ELHAM 2H **21**
Elham Ct. TN23: Ashf 1E **39**
                (off Matfield Cl.)
Elizabeth Carter Av. CT14: Deal 1D **10**
Elizabeth Dr. CT18: Cap F 3F **51**
Elizabeth Gdns. CT21: Hythe 6D **56**
Elizabeth Rd. CT17: Dover 5D **28**
Ellens Rd. CT14: Deal 2C **10**
Elling Rd. CT15: Alk 1D **24**
Ellingham Ind. Est. TN23: Ashf 2F **39**
Ellingham Way TN23: Ashf 2E **39**
Elm Ct. CT21: Hythe 6A **56**
Elmfield TN30: Tent 5B **64**
Elmfield Ct. TN30: Tent 6B **64**
Elmfield Pl. TN30: Tent 5B **64**
                 (off Elmfield)
Elm Gdns. CT21: Hythe 5G **57**
Elmhurst Cl. TN25: Ashf 1D **34**
Elm Pk. Gdns. CT17: Dover 4H **27**
Elm Pas. CT21: Hythe 5D **56**
Elm Pl. TN23: Ashf 5F **35**
Elm Rd. CT19: F'stone 1H **5** (1C **60**)
Elms Hill CT15: Hou 5E **27**
Elmstead Pl. CT20: F'stone 3H **5** (2C **60**)
Elms Va. Rd. CT15: Dover, Hou 5F **27**
  CT17: Dover 6A **6** (5F **27**)
Elventon Cl. CT19: F'stone 6E **49**
ELVINGTON 2E **49**
Elvington La. CT18: H'nge 2E **49**
Elwick La. TN23: Ashf 4B **4** (3F **35**)
Elwick Rd. TN23: Ashf 4A **4** (3F **35**)
Emmetts Cl. TN25: Mers 5H **39**
Emperor Way TN23: Kgnt 3D **38**
Emporia Cl. CT14: Deal 6E **9**

Enbrook Ct. CT20: F'stone 2F **59**
                (off Romney Av.)
Enbrook Rd. CT20: S'gte 2E **59**
Enbrook Valley CT20: F'stone 2E **59**
Encombe CT20: S'gte 4D **58**
Enfield Rd. CT14: Deal 4H **9**
Engineers Ct. TN23: Ashf 3A **4**
Enterprise Cen. TN24: Ashf 6H **35**
Enterprise Ho. TN25: Ashf 4E **31**
Eric Rd. CT17: Dover 1A **6** (1B **28**)
Erith St. CT17: Dover 1A **6** (2B **28**)
Ernwell Rd. CT19: F'stone 1G **5** (1B **60**)
Eshet Cl. TN23: Ashf 6E **35**
Esplanade CT17: Dover 5D **28**
Esplanade, The CT20: S'gte 5C **58**
Essella Pk. TN24: Ashf 4A **36**
Essella Rd. TN24: Ashf 4A **36**
Essetford Rd. TN23: Ashf 6D **34**
ETCHINGHILL 2F **47**
Etchinghill Golf Course 1E **47**
Ethelbert Rd. CT14: Deal 2G **9**
  CT17: Dover 3B **6** (3C **28**)
  CT19: F'stone 6B **50**
Ethelburga Dr. CT18: Lym'ge 4D **20**
Ethelburga Gro. CT18: Lym'ge 4D **20**
Ettrick Ter. CT21: Hythe 5C **56**
Eureka Bus. Pk. TN25: Ashf 4F **31**
Eureka Leisure Pk. TN25: Ashf 6F **31**
Eureka Pl. TN25: Ashf 4F **31**
Eureka Science Pk. TN25: Ashf 5F **31**
Eurogate Bus. Pk. TN24: Ashf 6E **31**
Eversley Ct. CT21: Hythe 4B **58**
Eversley Way CT20: F'stone 2F **59**
Evison Cl. CT16: Dover 1B **28**
EWELL MINNIS .6A **14**
Excalibur Cl. CT20: F'stone 3H **5**
Exchange St. CT14: Deal 4H **9**
Exeter Cl. CT19: F'stone 1D **58**
Exeter Ct. CT14: Walm 1H **11**
Exmoor Ri. TN24: Ashf 1F **35**
Exted Hill CT4: Elham 1G **21**
Eythorne Cl. TN24: Kenn 6H **31**

F

Fairfax Cl. CT20: F'stone 3D **58**
Fairfield CT4: Elham 1H **21**
  CT14: Shol 5D **8**
Fairings, The TN30: Tent 5B **64**
                 (off Ashford Rd.)
Fairlight Rd. CT21: Hythe 4C **56**
Fairview CT14: Lymp 4E **55**
Fairview Dr. TN24: W'boro 1H **39**
Fairview Gdns. CT14: Deal 3E **11**
Fairway, The CT14: Deal 3G **9**
Fairway CT19: F'stone 6G **49**
  CT21: Hythe 6E **57**
Fairway Av. CT19: F'stone 6G **49**
Falcon Way TN23: Ashf 6C **34**
Fan, The CT16: Dover 3H **29**
Farley Cl. TN26: Shad 5C **38**
Farm Cl. TN23: Ashf 6C **34**
Farmer Cl. CT17: Dover 4F **57**
Farmers Way TN23: Kgnt 2B **38**
Farm La. CT14: Shol 5D **8**
Farncombe Way CT16: Whitf 2B **16**
Farrers Wlk. TN23: Kgnt 3F **39**
Farrier Cl. TN25: Ashf 6D **30**
Farrier St. CT14: Deal 4H **9**
Farrow Ct. TN23: Ashf 1E **39**
FARTHING COMMON 6A **20**
FARTHINGLOE 5H **27**
Farthingloe Ct. CT17: Dover 5A **28**
Farthingloe Rd. CT17: Dover 6A **28**
Faustina Dr. TN23: Ashf 3D **38**
Faversham Rd. TN24: Kenn 3H **31**
  TN25: Bou A, Bou L, Kenn 2H **31**
Fenner Cl. CT20: F'stone 3E **59**
Fenton Ct. CT14: Deal 5F **9**
Ferdi Lethert Ho. TN24: Kenn 5A **32**
Ferguson Cl. CT21: Hythe 5H **57**

Fern Bank Cres. CT19: F'stone ...1G 5 (1B 60)
Fern Cl. CT18: H'nge ...5A 24
Fern Ct. CT16: Dover ...2E 7
Ferne La. CT15: Ewe M ...6A 14
Ferne Way CT20: F'stone ...1E 59
Fernfield CT18: H'nge ...5A 24
Fernfield La. CT18: H'nge ...5A 24
Fernley Ct. CT20: F'stone ...4F 5
Field End TN24: W'boro ...4B 36
Field Vw. TN23: Kgnt ...3E 39
Finch Gro. CT21: Hythe ...1H 63
Finch M. CT14: Deal ...1G 11
Findley Ct. CT21: Hythe ...5D 56
FINGLESHAM ...3A 8
Finn Farm Ct. TN23: Kgnt ...6H 39
Finn Farm Rd. TN23: Kgnt ...4F 39
　TN25: Mers ...5H 39
Fir Ct. TN24: W'boro ...4B 36
Firs, The CT14: Deal ...3H 9
Firs Cl. CT19: F'stone ...1D 58
Firs La. CT19: F'stone ...1D 58
Fisher Cl. CT21: Hythe ...6F 57
Fish Mkt. CT19: F'stone ...4H 5 (2C 60)
Fishmonger's La. CT16: Dover ...5E 7 (4E 29)
Fitness First
　Ashford ...3A 4 (3F 35)
Fitzwalter Ct. CT16: Dover ...5B 16
Fiveways Ri. CT14: Deal ...6D 8
Flanders Fld. TN25: Mers ...3G 41
Flaxpond Rd. TN23: Ashf ...6D 34
Fleet Rd. CT15: St Marg ...6E 13
Fleming Way CT19: F'stone ...5B 50
Fletchers Way CT14: Deal ...6E 9
Flimwell TN23: Ashf ...1B 38
Flodden Rd. CT14: Deal ...2D 10
Flood St. TN25: Mers ...6E 41
Florida Cl. CT14: Deal ...6B 16
Flying Horse La. CT16: Dover ...5F 7 (4E 29)
Focal Point Rd. CT16: Whitf ...5H 15
Foley Cl. TN24: Kenn ...6C 36
FOLKESTONE ...5G 5 (3B 60)
Folkestone Central Station (Rail) ...2H 59
Folkestone Ent. Cen. CT19: F'stone ...5F 49
Folkestone Invicta FC ...1G 59
Folkestone Mus. ...4G 5
Folkestone Racecourse ...1E 55
Folkestone Rd. CT15: Chu H, Dover ...1E 53
　CT17: Dover ...6A 6 (1E 53)
Folkestone Sports Cen. ...1H 59
Folkestone West Station (Rail) ...2F 59
Folkestone Yacht & Motorboat Club ...4H 5
Folks Wood Way CT21: Lymp ...4E 55
Folly Rd. CT20: F'stone ...1C 60
FOORD ...1G 5 (1B 60)
Foord Rd. CT19: F'stone ...2F 5 (1B 60)
　CT20: F'stone ...3F 5 (1B 60)
Foord Rd. Sth. CT20: F'stone ...4G 5 (2B 60)
Ford Way TN23: Ashf ...4D 34
Fore Cotts. TN23: Gt Cha ...4A 34
Foreland Av. CT19: F'stone ...1D 60
Foreland Ct. CT15: St Marg ...4E 19
Foreland Rd. CT15: St Marg ...4E 19
Forelands Sq. CT14: Deal ...2F 11
Forestall Mdw. TN23: Kgnt ...3F 39
Forest Av. TN25: Ashf ...6C 30
Forester's Way CT16: Dover ...4F 5 (2B 60)
Forge Cl. TN25: S'ndge ...4B 44
Forge Fld. CT15: W Hou ...6A 26
Forge La. CT16: Whitf ...1H 15
　TN23: Ashf ...3A 4 (3F 35)
Forge Path CT16: Whitf ...1A 16
Forrester Pl. TN23: Ashf ...5G 35
Forson Cl. TN30: Tent ...5B 64
FORSTAL, THE ...4F 41
Forstal, The TN25: Wye ...1G 33
Fort Burgoyne Rd. CT16: Gus ...1G 7 (2E 29)
Fortescue Pl. TN25: Sme ...2E 43
Fort Rd. CT21: Hythe ...5C 56
Forum Way TN23: Kgnt ...2C 38
Fostall Grn. TN23: Ashf ...6D 34
Foster Rd. TN24: Svgtn ...6C 36
Fosters Cl. CT19: F'stone ...6E 49
Foster Way CT14: Deal ...6F 9
Fougeres Way TN24: Ashf ...1E 35
Fountains Cl. TN24: W'boro ...4C 36
Fowlmead Country Pk. ...3C 8
Fowlmead Country Pk. Vis. Cen. ...3C 8
Fox Cl. CT18: Lym'ge ...4D 20
Foxglove Grn. TN24: W'boro ...3A 36

Foxglove Rd. TN24: W'boro ...4A 36
Fox Holt Rd. CT15: S'fld ...1G 23
Foys Pas. CT21: Hythe ...5E 57
Frampton Rd. CT21: Hythe ...5C 56
France Rd. CT16: Whitf ...4A 16
Francis Rd. TN23: Ashf ...5F 35
Frank Edinger Cl. TN24: Kenn ...1H 35
Fraser Way CT18: H'nge ...2F 49
Freathy La. TN25: Kenn ...3G 31
Frederick Benn Pl. TN23: Ashf ...2D 34
Frederick Ct. CT14: Deal ...2E 11
Freedown, The CT15: St Marg ...2E 19
Freemen's Way CT14: Deal ...2F 11
Fremantle Rd. CT20: F'stone ...2E 59
Freshfield La. CT21: Salt ...5E 57
Friar's Way CT16: Dover ...6A 16
Friends Cl. CT14: Deal ...4G 9
Friesian Way TN24: Kenn ...4G 31
Frinsted Gdns. TN23: Ashf ...1C 38
Frith Rd. CT16: Dover ...2C 6 (2C 28)
Frittenden Cl. TN23: Ashf ...1C 38
FROGHOLT ...6H 47
Front, The CT15: St Marg ...6E 19
Front St. CT14: R'wld ...2D 12
Fulbert Rd. CT16: Dover ...4B 16
Fulmar Ct. CT16: Dover ...2D 6 (2D 28)
Fulmar M. CT18: H'nge ...2G 49
Furley Cl. TN24: Kenn ...4H 31
Fusilier Av. CT20: F'stone ...2B 58

G

Gainsborough Cl. CT19: F'stone ...6G 49
Gala Bingo
　Dover ...4E 7
Galahad Way CT16: Whitf ...4A 16
Gallagher Retail Pk. TN23: Ashf ...6F 35
Galloway Dr. TN24: Kenn ...3G 31
Gallow's Cnr. CT21: Hythe ...5C 56
Gaol La. CT17: Dover ...5E 7
Garden Ho. Ct. CT20: F'stone ...3H 59
Garden M. CT14: Walm ...3E 11
Garden Pl. TN24: Kenn ...5A 32
Garden Rd. CT19: F'stone ...2F 5 (1B 60)
Garden Wlk. CT14: Deal ...4G 9
Gardner Cl. CT18: H'nge ...2F 49
Garton Way TN23: Ashf ...6A 34
Gasworks La. TN23: Ashf ...4A 4 (3F 35)
　(not continuous)
Gateway, The CT16: Dover ...5G 7 (4E 29)
Gateway to the White Cliffs ...2G 29
Gaunt's Cl. CT14: Deal ...1E 11
Geddes Cl. CT18: H'nge ...2F 49
George All. CT14: Deal ...5H 9
George Cooper Ho. CT20: F'stone ...6E 5
George Gurr Cres. CT19: F'stone ...5B 50
George La. CT20: F'stone ...5G 5 (3B 60)
George Stone Ho. CT20: F'stone ...4H 5
George St. CT14: Deal ...4H 9
　CT17: Dover ...1A 6 (2B 28)
　TN23: Ashf ...6B 4 (4F 35)
George Williams Way TN24: Kenn ...1H 35
Geraldine Rd. CT19: F'stone ...1F 59
Gerald Palmby Ct. CT14: Deal ...4G 9
Gerlach Ho. TN24: Kenn ...6G 31
GIBBONS BROOK ...3D 44
GIBRALTAR ...3F 49
Gibraltar La. CT18: H'nge ...2E 49
Gibraltar Sq. CT15: Gus ...6E 17
Gilbert Pl. CT20: S'gte ...4E 59
Gilbert Rd. TN23: Ashf ...3B 4 (4F 35)
Gilford Rd. CT14: Deal ...6G 9
Gilham Gro. CT14: Deal ...1F 11
Gill La. TN25: Mers ...6C 40
Gillman Cl. CT18: H'nge ...1F 49
Glack Rd. CT14: Deal ...1D 10
Glade, The CT14: Shol ...5D 8
Gladstone Rd. CT14: Deal, Walm ...1G 11
　CT19: F'stone ...1H 5 (1C 60)
　TN24: W'boro ...3A 40
Glebe Cl. CT15: St Marg ...3D 18
Glebelands CT15: Alk ...2H 25
　(not continuous)
　TN25: Mers ...3G 41
Glebe Way TN24: Kenn ...4H 31
Glendale CT20: F'stone ...5H 5
Glenfield Rd. CT16: Dover ...6B 16
Glen Gro. CT17: Dover ...5A 6 (4B 28)

Glenmore Centre, The CT16: Whitf ...4C 16
　TN24: Ashf ...1B 40
Glen Rd. CT14: Kgdn, Walm ...1G 13
Glenwood TN30: St Mic ...2B 64
Glenwood Cl. TN30: St Mic ...2B 64
Gloster Cl. CT18: H'nge ...2H 49
Gloster Ropewalk CT17: Dover ...6C 28
Gloster Ter. CT20: S'gte ...5D 58
Gloster Way CT17: Dover ...6C 28
Gloucester Pl. CT20: F'stone ...4G 5 (2B 60)
Glover Rd. TN24: W'boro ...4A 36
GOAT LEES ...3G 31
Goat Lees La. TN25: Kenn ...3H 31
Goatmans Yd. CT4: Elham ...1H 21
Godfrey Marchant Gro. TN23: Ashf ...2C 34
Godfrey Wlk. TN23: Ashf ...5F 35
Godinton House & Gardens ...1A 34
Godinton La. TN23: Ashf, Gt Cha ...6A 30
　TN26: Hoth ...6B 30
Godinton Park ...1A 34
Godinton Rd. TN23: Ashf ...4B 4 (3F 35)
　(Bank St.)
　TN23: Ashf ...3A 4 (3E 35)
　(Godinton Way)
Godinton Way TN23: Ashf ...3A 4 (3E 35)
Godinton Way Ind. Est.
　TN23: Ashf ...4A 4 (3F 35)
Godwin Ct. TN23: Kgnt ...2B 38
Godwin Rd. CT16: Dover ...3H 7 (3F 29)
Godwyne Cl. CT16: Dover ...3E 7 (3D 28)
Godwyne Ct. CT16: Dover ...2E 7 (2D 28)
Godwyne Path CT16: Dover ...2E 7 (2D 28)
Godwyne Rd. CT16: Dover ...3E 7 (3D 28)
Godwyn Gdns. CT20: F'stone ...3G 59
Godwyn Rd. CT14: Deal ...3G 9
　CT20: F'stone ...2G 59
Golden Sq. TN30: Tent ...5B 64
Golden St. CT14: Deal ...4H 9
Goldings Ct. TN24: Kenn ...1G 35
Goldsmith Cl. TN30: Tent ...4B 64
Golf Ct. CT14: Deal ...2G 9
Golf Rd. CT14: Deal ...1G 9
Goodcheap La. TN25: Hin ...6E 33
Goodfellow Way CT16: Dover ...3D 6 (3D 28)
Good Hope Cl. TN24: Deal ...1D 10
Goodwin Cl. CT14: Deal ...2E 11
Goodwin Rd. CT15: St Marg ...5D 18
Gordon Cl. TN24: Ashf ...3H 35
Gordon Rd. CT16: Whitf ...4A 16
　CT20: F'stone ...1D 58
Gore Ct. TN24: Ashf ...1C 4
Gore Hill TN24: Ashf ...1C 4 (1G 35)
Gorley Ho. CT17: Dover ...5E 7 (4D 28)
Gorse Mead TN23: Ashf ...5D 34
Goschen Ct. CT17: Dover ...3A 6 (3B 28)
Goteley Mere TN24: Kenn ...4G 31
Gothic Ct. CT14: Walm ...4F 11
Gothic Cotts. TN23: Gt Cha ...4A 34
Gough Rd. CT20: S'gte ...4E 59
Grace Ct. CT20: F'stone ...4G 5
Grace Hill CT20: F'stone ...4G 5 (2B 60)
Grace Mdw. CT16: Whitf ...2H 15
Grace Wlk. CT14: Deal ...6E 9
Grampion Cl. TN24: Ashf ...1C 4 (1G 35)
Gram's Rd. CT14: Walm ...4F 11
Granary Ct. Rd. TN25: Sme ...2G 43
Grand Ct. CT20: F'stone ...4H 59
　(off Earls Av.)
Grand Shaft ...5D 28
Grange Ct. CT20: F'stone ...5E 5
Grange Cres. TN30: St Mic ...2A 64
Grange Rd. CT14: Deal ...6F 9
　CT19: F'stone ...1E 59
　CT21: Salt ...3D 56
　TN30: St Mic ...2A 64
Grantham Av. CT14: Deal ...6E 9
Grantley Cl. TN23: Ashf ...6E 35
Granville Pde. CT20: S'gte ...4E 59
Granville Rd. CT14: Kgdn ...4H 13
　CT14: Walm ...3G 11
　CT15: St Marg ...4E 19
Granville Rd. E. CT20: S'gte ...4F 59
Granville Rd. W. CT20: S'gte ...4E 59
Granville St. CT14: Deal ...6H 9
　CT16: Dover ...2C 6 (2C 28)
Grasmere Gdns. CT19: F'stone ...6H 49
Grasmere Rd. TN24: Kenn ...5G 31
Grasslands TN23: Ashf ...6B 34
Gravel La. CT15: Chu H, W Hou ...1B 52

Gravelly Fld. TN23: Ashf 5A 34
Gravel Wlk. TN23: Ashf 2A 4
Gray Cl. CT18: H'nge 6H 23
Graylen Cl. CT14: Deal 4G 9
Gt. Burton Ho's. *TN24: Kenn* 6A 32
(off Nettlefield)
GREAT CHART 4A 34
Gt. Chart By-Pass TN23: Ashf, Gt Cha 5A 34
Gt. Conduit St. CT21: Hythe 5E 57
Great Fishers TN23: Ashf 6A 34
GREAT MONGEHAM 2B 10
Great Oak Row TN23: Kgnt 3F 39
Grebe Cl. CT18: H'nge 1G 49
Grebe Cres. CT21: Hythe 1G 63
Green, The CT21: Salt 3D 56
 TN25: Wye 1G 33
 TN29: Burm 5A 62
Greenacre Dr. CT14: Walm 4G 11
Greenbank TN24: Kenn 5H 31
Greenbanks CT18: Lym'ge 5E 21
Green Cl. CT16: Whitf 4A 16
 CT18: H'nge 1H 49
Green Ct. CT19: F'stone 6C 50
Greencroft TN23: Ashf 1B 38
Greenfield Cotts. TN25: S'ndge 3C 44
Greenfield Rd. CT19: F'stone 1H 5 (6C 50)
Greenfields TN25: S'ndge 3C 44
Green Flds. La. TN23: Ashf 6B 34
Greengates CT16: Whitf 1A 16
Green La. CT4: R Min 2A 20
 CT14: Walm 4F 11
 CT15: Alk, Ewe M ....1G 25 & 6A 14
 CT15: St Marg 1C 18
 CT16: Dover 1B 28
 CT16: Temp E, Whitf 4F 15
(not continuous)
 CT18: Cap F 2F 51
 CT19: F'stone 1H 5 (1C 60)
 CT21: Hythe 5C 56
 TN23: Ashf 2C 38
Green La. Av. CT21: Hythe 5B 56
Greenwich Cl. CT15: Ewe M 5A 14
Gregory Ct. TN25: Wye 1G 33
Gregory Ho. *CT17: Dover* 3B 6
(off East St.)
Grenadier Way TN23: Ashf 5A 34
Greville Ho. CT17: Dover 6B 6
Greyhound Chase TN23: Ashf 6B 34
Greystones TN24: W'boro 4B 36
Grey Willow Gdns. TN23: Ashf 5B 34
Grice Cl. CT18: H'nge 2F 49
Griffin Cl. TN23: Ashf 5A 34
Griffin St. CT14: Deal 4H 9
Grimston Av. CT20: F'stone 2H 59
Grimston Gdns. CT20: F'stone 3H 59
Grosvenor Rd. TN24: Kenn 4G 31
Grosvenor Ter. *CT20: F'stone* 1C 60
(off The Tram Rd.)
Grove, The CT14: Deal 5G 9
 CT16: Dover 1B 6 (2C 28)
 CT21: Hythe 5E 57
 TN24: Kenn 5A 32
Grove Bri. TN25: S'ndge 5B 44
Grove Ct. CT20: F'stone 2H 5 (1C 60)
Grove Rd. CT14: Walm 2H 11
 CT20: F'stone 2H 5 (1C 60)
Guernsey Way TN24: Kenn 4G 31
Guildhall Ct. CT20: F'stone 4F 5
Guildhall St. CT20: F'stone 4G 5 (2B 60)
Guildhall St. Nth. CT20: F'stone 3F 5 (2B 60)
Guilford Av. CT16: Whitf 1H 15
Guilford Ct. CT14: Walm 3H 11
Gurling Rd. CT15: St Marg 6D 12
GUSTON 3E 17
Guston La. CT15: E Lan 1F 17
Guston Rd. CT15: E Lan 1G 17
 CT16: Dover 1F 7 (1E 29)
Guthrie Gdns. CT17: Dover 6G 15

H

Hackfield TN23: Ashf 4D 34
HACKLINGE 1A 4
Hacklinge Rd. CT14: Hackl, Worth 1A 4
Hadleigh Cl. TN25: Mers 5H 39
Hadrian Gdns. TN23: Kgnt 2D 38
Haffenden Rd. TN30: Tent 4A 64
Hafod Pas. CT21: Hythe 5E 57

Hagger Dr. CT18: H'nge 6A 24
Hales Cl. TN30: Tent 5B 64
Hales Ct. TN30: Tent 5B 64
Hall Av. TN24: Ashf, Svgtn 1B 40
Hall Cres. CT14: Shol 6D 8
Halliday Ct. CT21: Hythe 5C 56
Halliday Dr. CT14: Walm 2G 11
Halstatt Rd. CT14: Deal 2E 11
Halstow Way TN23: Ashf 5D 34
Halt, The CT4: Elham 2H 21
Hamilton Rd. CT14: Deal 1F 11
 CT17: Dover 3A 28
 TN24: W'boro 1H 39
Hammonds Rd. CT20: F'stone 2E 59
Hampden La. TN23: Ashf 6E 35
Hampden M. TN23: Ashf 1E 39
Hampden Rd. TN23: Ashf 1E 39
Hampton Va. CT21: Hythe 3B 58
Hancocks Fld. CT14: Deal 6E 9
Hangmans La. CT14: Ripp 2B 12
 CT14: R'wld 2D 12
 CT15: Gus 3F 17
Hanover Cl. CT14: Walm 3H 11
 TN23: Ashf 3D 34
Hanover Ct. CT21: Hythe 6E 57
(off Court App.)
Harbour App. Rd. CT20: F'stone 5H 5 (3C 60)
Harbour Ct. CT20: F'stone 3H 5
Harbourne La. TN26: H Hald 1D 64
 TN30: St Mic, H Hald 1D 64
Harbour Point CT19: F'stone 2C 60
Harbour St. CT20: F'stone 4H 5 (2C 60)
Harbour Vw. Rd. CT17: Dover 3A 6 (3B 28)
Harbour Way CT20: F'stone 3H 5 (2C 60)
Harcourt Rd. CT19: F'stone 6F 49
Hardinge Rd. TN24: Ashf 2C 4 (2G 35)
Hardwicke Rd. CT17: Dover 5B 28
Hardwick Rd. CT20: F'stone 3G 59
Hardy Cl. TN24: W'boro 6C 36
Hardy Rd. CT15: St Marg 1C 18
Harleighbury Rd. CT15: St Marg 3D 18
Harman Av. CT21: Lymp 4D 54
Harold Pas. CT16: Dover 4F 7 (3E 29)
Harold Rd. CT14: Deal 3G 9
Harold's Rd. CT16: Dover 3G 7 (3E 29)
Harold St. CT16: Dover 3E 7 (3D 28)
(not continuous)
Harper Rd. TN23: Ashf 5D 34
Harpswood La. CT21: Hythe 4C 56
Harrier Cl. CT18: H'nge 2G 49
Harringe La. TN25: S'ndge 6G 43
Harriot Cl. CT19: F'stone 6H 49
Harrow Way TN23: Kgnt 2C 38
Harry Pay Cl. TN24: Kenn 1A 36
Hart Cl. CT18: H'nge 1G 49
Harvest Cotts. TN25: Sme 2D 42
Harvest Way CT18: H'nge 1H 49
 TN23: Ashf 6B 34
Harvey Av. CT14: Walm 2G 11
Harvey Ho. CT20: F'stone 3H 5 (2C 60)
Harvey Pl. CT20: F'stone 3H 5
(Harvey St.)
 CT20: F'stone 2A 6 (2B 60)
(The Old High St.)
Harvey Rd. TN24: W'boro 4B 36
Harvey St. CT20: F'stone 3H 5 (2C 60)
Harville Rd. TN25: Bou A, Wye 1C 32
Harwood Rd. TN25: Wye 1G 33
Hasborough Rd. CT19: F'stone 1D 60
Haskard Cl. CT18: H'nge 1F 49
Havelock Rd. CT14: Walm 2G 11
Haven, The CT21: Hythe 6G 55
 TN23: Kgnt 2D 38
Haven Dr. CT18: H'nge 1G 49
Haventhorpe TN24: Kenn 1B 4 (2F 35)
Havillands Pl. TN25: Wye 1F 33
Hawkesbury St. CT17: Dover 6D 28
HAWKINGE 1H 49
Hawkinge Cemetery & Crematorium
 CT18: H'nge 6F 23
Hawkins Rd. CT19: F'stone 1D 58
HAWKSDOWN 5F 11
Hawksdown Rd. CT14: Walm 5F 11
Hawkshill Camp Rd. CT14: Walm 6G 11
Hawkshill Rd. CT14: Walm 5G 11
Hawks Way TN23: Ashf 6C 34
Hawthorn Cl. CT21: Hythe 6A 56

Hawthorne Cl. CT17: Dover 1G 27
Hawthorn Farm CT15: Mart M 6A 12
Hawthorn Rd. TN23: Kgnt 3F 39
Haymakers La. TN23: Ashf 5B 34
Hayton Rd. TN25: Stanf 2D 44
Haywain Cl. TN23: Kgnt 2C 38
Hayward Cl. CT14: Deal 1E 11
 TN24: W'boro 5C 36
Hazeldown Cl. CT17: Dover 1G 27
Hazel Hgts. TN25: Ashf 6C 30
Heartwood Dr. TN23: Ashf 2C 34
Heath Ct. CT15: St Marg 3D 18
Heather Dr. TN30: St Mic 2B 64
Heathfield Av. CT16: Dover 1B 28
Heathfield Ct. TN24: Ashf 1C 4
Heathfield Rd. TN24: Ashf 1D 4 (2G 35)
Hedgerows TN23: Ashf 6B 34
Hedgers Way TN23: Kgnt 2B 38
Heights Ter. CT17: Dover 5C 28
Helena Corniche CT20: S'gte 4C 58
Helena Rd. CT18: Cap F 3G 51
Helena Vs. CT17: Dover 4B 58
Hempton Hill TN25: M Hor 1G 45
HEMSTED 3A 20
Hengist Rd. CT14: Deal 4H 9
Henley Flds. TN30: St Mic 3B 64
Henley Mdws. TN30: Tent 3A 64
Henley Vw. TN30: St Mic 3B 64
Henniker Cl. CT16: Whitf 4H 15
Henwood TN24: Ashf 2H 35
Henwood Bus. Cen. TN24: Ashf 2H 35
Henwood Ind. Est. TN24: Ashf 2H 35
Herbert Rd. TN24: W'boro 1H 39
Herbert St. CT17: Dover 1A 6 (2B 28)
Herdson Rd. CT20: F'stone 2G 59
Herdwick Cl. TN25: Mers 5H 39
Hereford Cl. TN24: Kenn 4G 31
Heritage Gdns. CT16: Dover 3F 7 (3E 29)
Heritage Rd. CT20: F'stone 1D 58
Hermitage Cl. CT21: Hythe 5D 56
Heron Bus. Cen. TN24: Ashf 2H 35
Heron Forstal Av. CT18: H'nge 1H 49
Heron Ho. TN23: Ashf 4D 34
Heron Lodge CT16: Dover 1B 28
Heron's Brook TN25: Brook 5F 33
Heron's Way CT21: Hythe 1G 63
Heron Wlk. TN23: Ashf 5C 34
Herschell Rd. E. CT14: Walm 2G 11
Herschell Rd. W. CT14: Walm 2G 11
Herschell Sq. CT14: Walm 2G 11
Hestia Way TN23: Kgnt 2C 38
Hever Gdns. TN23: Ashf 2D 38
Hewitt Rd. CT16: Dover 3D 6 (3D 28)
Hewitts Pl. TN24: W'boro 4B 36
Hextable Cl. TN23: Ashf 1D 38
Heyford Cl. CT18: H'nge 1H 49
Highbury La. TN30: Tent 6A 64
Highfield Cl. CT21: Salt 3C 56
Highfield Ind. Est. CT19: F'stone 1D 60
Highfield La. TN24: Svgtn 2D 40
 TN25: Mers 2D 40
Highfield Rd. TN24: W'boro 5C 36
Highland Cl. CT20: F'stone 3F 59
High Meadow 2A 6 (2B 28)
High Mdw. CT17: Dover 2B 6 (2C 28)
Highpoint Bus. Village TN24: Ashf 2H 35
High Ridge CT21: Hythe 4A 58
 TN23: Ashf 6A 34
High St. CT4: Elham 2H 21
 CT14: Deal 4H 9
 CT15: St Marg 3D 18
 CT16: Dover 3C 6 (3C 28)
 CT16: Temp E 4F 15
 CT18: Lym'ge 5D 20
 CT21: Hythe 5D 56
 TN24: Ashf 3B 4 (3F 35)
(not continuous)
 TN25: Wye 1G 33
 TN30: Tent 6A 64
High Trees Cl. TN24: W'boro 4C 35
Highview Pk. CT18: Cap F 5E 51
Hillbrow La. TN23: Ashf 4D 34
Hillbrow Rd. TN23: Ashf 5E 35
Hillcrest TN23: Gt Cha 5A 34
Hillcrest Cl. TN24: Kenn 5A 32
Hillcrest Gdns. CT14: Walm 3E 11
Hillcrest Rd. CT14: Kgdn 3G 13
 CT21: Hythe 4D 56
Hill La. CT18: Peene 5B 48

Hill Ri. TN25: Ashf 6C 30
Hill Rd. CT19: F'stone 5B 50
Hillside CT20: S'gte 4E 59
Hillside Ct. CT21: Hythe 5E 57
Hillside Ind. Est. CT20: F'stone 3E 59
Hillside Rd. CT17: Dover 1A 28
Hillside St. CT21: Hythe 5D 56
Hill Vw. TN24: Ashf 1D 4 (2G 35)
          (not continuous)
Hillyfields Rd. TN23: Ashf 5E 35
Hillyfields Ri. TN23: Ashf 4E 35
Hilton Bus. Cen. TN23: Ashf 1F 39
Hilton Rd. TN23: Ashf 3D 34
HINXHILL 3F 37
Hinxhill Rd. TN24: Hin, W'boro 5E 37
   TN25: Hin 5E 37
Hirst Cl. CT17: Dover 5B 16
HM Immigration Removal Centre Dover
   CT17: Dover 5B 28
Hoads Wood Gdns. TN25: Ashf 5C 30
Hobart Cres. CT16: Dover 6B 16
HOCKLEY SOLE 6E 25
Hockley Sole CT18: Cap F 6D 24
Hockley Sole La. CT18: Cap F 6E 25
Hogben Cl. CT18: Lym'ge 4D 20
Hogbrook Hill La. CT15: Alk 2H 25
Hog Grn. CT4: Elham 2H 21
Holdenhurst TN23: Ashf 1C 38
Hollands Av. CT19: F'stone 6D 50
Hollands Hill CT15: Mart M 6A 12
Hollington Pl. TN24: Ashf 2B 4 (2F 35)
Hollow Wood Rd. CT17: Dover 3G 27
Holly Cl. CT19: F'stone 6C 50
   CT21: Hythe 4F 57
Holly Mdws. TN23: Ashf 2B 34
Holmesdale Ter. CT20: F'stone 5F 5
Holmestone Rd. CT17: Dover 2G 27
Holmlea Cl. TN24: W'boro 4B 36
Holmwood Rd. TN23: Ashf 6C 34
Holt Cl. TN23: Ashf 5A 34
Holywell Av. CT19: F'stone 5A 50
Holywell Ho. CT19: F'stone 5A 50
Homefield Av. CT14: Deal 5F 9
Homefield Row CT14: Deal 5F 9
Homelands Cl. TN25: S'ndge 4B 44
Homemead La. CT14: Hackl 2A 8
Homepeak Ho. CT21: Hythe 5D 56
      (off Bartholomew St.)
Homepine Ho. CT20: F'stone 3A 60
Homestead TN23: Ashf 5B 34
Homestead Ct. CT14: Deal 1E 11
Homevale Ho's. CT20: S'gte 4E 59
Homewood Rd. TN30: Tent 4B 64
Honeyfield TN23: Ashf 4C 34
Honeywood CT21: S'lng 6H 45
Honeywood Cl. CT16: Whitf 3A 16
   CT21: Lymp 3E 55
Honeywood Parkway CT16: Gus, Whitf . .4A 16
Honeywood Rd. CT16: Whitf 3A 16
Honner Cl. CT18: H'nge 2F 49
Hook Cl. CT20: F'stone 2F 59
Hope Cotts. TN25: Bra L 1E 43
Hope Rd. CT14: Deal 6H 9
Hoppers Way TN23: Ashf 5B 34
Horizon CT21: Hythe 5H 57
Hornash La. TN26: Shad 5D 38
Hornbeam Cl. TN23: Ashf 2D 34
HORN STREET 3B 58
Horn St. CT19: F'stone 2B 58
   CT20: F'stone 2B 58
   CT21: Hythe 4B 58
Horsa Rd. CT14: Deal 3H 9
Horsley Cl. CT18: H'nge 2H 49
Hospital Hill CT21: Hythe 4B 58
Hotel Rd. CT15: St Marg 3F 19
HOTHFIELD .1D 30
Hougham Ct. La. CT15: Chu H 2C 52
Hougham Top Rd. CT15: Chu H 1C 52
Houghton Ho. CT19: F'stone 2A 60
Housefield TN24: W'boro 3B 36
House Mdw. TN23: Ashf 6A 34
Howe Rd. CT15: St Marg 1D 18
Hoxton Cl. TN23: Ashf 5A 34
Hubert Pas. CT16: Dover 4F 7 (3E 29)
Hudson Cl. CT16: Dover 6B 16
Hughes Cotts. TN25: Sme 2D 42
Hull Pl. CT14: Shol 5D 8
Hume Ct. CT21: Hythe 6F 57
Huncourt Pl. CT20: F'stone 4G 5

Hunt Cl. CT18: H'nge 1G 49
Hunter Av. TN24: W'boro 5A 36
Hunter Cl. TN24: W'boro 5A 36
Hunter Rd. TN24: W'boro 4A 36
Hunters Bank CT4: Elham 2H 21
Hunters Wlk. CT14: Deal 5E 9
Huntswood TN23: Ashf 5C 34
Huron Ter. CT16: Dover 6B 16
        (off Green La.)
Hurricane Way CT18: H'nge 2G 49
Hurst La. CT18: Cap F 1F 51
Hurst Rd. TN24: Kenn 4F 31
        (not continuous)
Hyde Ct. CT17: Dover 6B 6 (4C 28)
HYTHE 5E 57
Hythe & Saltwood Sailing Club 6E 57
        (off Marine Pde.)
Hythe Cl. CT20: F'stone 2F 59
Hythe Imperial Golf Course 5G 57
Hythe Local History Room 5E 57
Hythe Rd. CT21: Ped 2F 55
   TN24: Ashf, W'boro 3H 35
        (not continuous)
   TN25: Mers, S'ndge, Sme 5E 37
   TN29: Dym 6D 62
Hythe Station
   Romney, Hythe & Dymchurch Railway
   . . . . .5C 56
Hythe Swimming Pool 6F 57
Hyton Cl. CT14: Deal 5F 9
Hyton Dr. CT14: Deal 5F 9

I

Ian's Wlk. CT21: Hythe 4A 58
Ilex Rd. CT19: F'stone 1F 59
Imperial Way TN23: Ashf 5A 34
INGLEDEN 3D 64
Ingleden Cotts. TN30: Tent 2C 64
Ingleden Pk. Rd. TN30: Tent 4B 64
        (not continuous)
Ingles La. CT20: F'stone 3E 5 (2A 60)
Ingles M. CT20: F'stone 5E 5 (3A 60)
Ingles Rd. CT20: F'stone 5E 5 (3A 60)
Ingles Way CT20: F'stone 4F 5 (2B 60)
Ingleton Wood Rd. CT15: Dover, Hou . . .5H 25
Ingoldsby Rd. CT19: F'stone 6C 50
Ingram Cl. CT18: H'nge 2F 49
Intelligence Wlk. TN23: Ashf 1D 34
International Ho. TN23: Ashf 5D 4 (4G 35)
Invicta Rd. CT19: F'stone 6B 50
Inward Car Lanes CT16: Dover 3G 29
Inward Freight Lanes CT16: Dover 3G 29
Ireland Ter. TN23: Ashf 1E 39
Irene Astor Ct. CT20: F'stone 3G 5
Isis Bus. Cen. TN24: Ashf 1A 40
Isis Bus. Pk. TN24: Ashf 1A 40
Isis Cl. CT21: Lymp 4E 55
Ivy Cl. CT18: Etch'l 2F 47
Ivy Cotts. TN23: Ashf 3A 4 (3F 35)
   TN23: Gt Cha 5A 34
Ivy Ct. TN30: Tent 6B 64
Ivy Pl. CT14: Deal 4H 9
Ivy Way CT19: F'stone 6C 50

J

Jack Dunbar Pl. TN23: Ashf 2C 34
Jacksons La. TN30: Tent 6A 64
Jacobs Ct. TN25: Mers 5H 39
Jacobs Oak TN24: W'boro 1H 39
James Allchin Gdns. TN24: Kenn 1B 36
James Cl. CT18: Lym'ge 4D 20
James Ct. CT20: F'stone 3G 59
James Ewart Av. TN23: Ashf 2D 34
James Hall Gdns. CT14: Walm 2G 11
James Haney Dr. TN24: Kenn 6B 32
James Ho. CT16: Dover 1D 6
James St. CT19: F'stone 1G 5 (6C 50)
   TN23: Ashf 3E 35
Jarman's Fld. TN25: Wye 1H 33
Jarrett Ho. CT20: F'stone 6E 5 (3A 60)
Jarvis Dr. TN24: W'boro 6C 36
Jarvis Pl. TN30: St Mic 2B 64
Jarvist Pl. CT14: Kgdn 1H 13
Javelin Ent. Pk. TN24: Ashf 2A 36
Javelin Way TN24: Ashf 2A 36

Jaynes Ind. Estate, The CT17: Dover 3G 27
Jefferson Cl. TN23: Ashf 4D 34
Jellicoe Cl. TN24: W'boro 6C 36
Jemmett Rd. TN23: Ashf 6A 4 (6E 35)
Jersey Cl. TN24: Kenn 3G 31
Jesmond St. CT19: F'stone 2F 5 (1B 60)
Jillian Way TN23: Ashf 6C 34
Joem Gallery .6H 9
        (off Victoria Rd.)
Johannesburg Rd. CT16: Dover 5C 16
John Badger Cl. TN24: Kenn 6A 32
John Coulthard Dr. TN23: Ashf 2D 34
John Dutton Way TN24: Kenn 1A 36
John Myers Sports Hall 3F 11
John Newington Cl. TN24: Kenn 6B 32
Johnson Cl. TN24: W'boro 6C 36
John Tapping Cl. CT14: Walm 4F 11
Jointon Rd. CT20: F'stone 3H 59
Jonathan Ho. CT16: Dover 2D 6
Joseph Hadlum Ct. TN23: Ashf 3A 4
Joyes Cl. CT16: Whitf 2B 16
   CT19: F'stone 6C 50
Joyes Rd. CT16: Whitf 2A 16
   CT19: F'stone 6B 50
Jubilee Cl. CT21: Hythe 1H 63
Jubilee Dr. CT14: Walm 2H 11
Jubilee Way CT15: Gus, Whitf 3A 16
   CT16: Dover 3G 29
   CT16: Dover, Whitf 3A 16
Julian Rd. CT19: F'stone 2H 59
Julien Pl. TN24: W'boro 5C 36
Julie Rose Stadium, The 1B 36
Juniper Cl. TN23: Ashf 3C 34
Jupiter La. TN23: Kgnt 2C 38

K

Kathleen M. CT20: F'stone 4G 5
KEARSNEY 5G 15
Kearsney Av. CT16: Dover 5G 15
Kearsney Ct. CT16: Temp E 5E 15
Kearsney Station (Rail) 5F 15
Keddow's Cl. CT21: Hythe 1H 63
Kedleston Rd. CT16: Whitf 4B 16
Keepers La. CT18: Acr 2A 22
Kelvedon Rd. CT14: Walm 3G 11
KEMPE'S CORNER 1C 32
Kempes Pl. TN25: Wye 1G 33
        (off Upper Bri. St.)
Kenbrook TN24: Kenn 4G 31
Kengate Ind. Est. CT21: Hythe 6B 56
Kenilworth Cl. CT15: St Marg 3E 19
Kennard Way TN24: Ashf 3A 36
Kennedy Dr. CT14: Walm 3F 11
Kennet La. TN25: Stanf 4E 45
Kennett Dr. CT14: Deal 3E 11
KENNINGTON 4H 31
Kennington Pl. TN24: Kenn 4H 31
Kennington Rd. TN24: W'boro 2C 36
Kent & East Sussex Railway
   Tenterden Town Station 5A 64
Kent Av. TN24: Ashf 2A 4 (2F 35)
Kent Battle of Britain Mus. 1F 49
Kent Ho. CT20: F'stone 3H 59
Kent Rd. CT19: F'stone 6E 49
Kestrel Cl. TN23: Kgnt 4G 39
Kestrel Ct. CT16: Dover 6B 16
Kestrel Wlk. CT18: H'nge 2F 49
Kettle Dr. CT18: H'nge 6H 23
Keyes Cl. CT16: Whitf 4A 16
Keyes Pl. CT17: F'stone 5C 50
Keys, The CT18: H'nge 6A 24
Khartoum Sq. CT16: Whitf 4A 16
Kilndown Cl. TN23: Ashf 1C 38
Kiln Fld. TN30: Tent 6C 64
Kimberley Cl. CT16: Dover 6C 16
Kimberley Ter. CT18: Lym'ge 4E 21
Kimberley Wlk. CT16: Dover 5C 16
Kimberley Way TN23: Ashf 6G 35
   TN24: Ashf 6G 35
King Charles Ct. CT14: Walm 3H 11
King Edward Rd. CT14: Deal 3H 9
Kingfisher Av. CT21: Hythe 1G 63
Kingfisher Bus. Cen. TN23: Ashf 2H 35
Kingfisher Cl. CT16: Svgtn 6C 16
Kingfisher Gdns. CT21: Hythe 1G 63
Kingfisher Ho. TN23: Ashf 4D 34
King Lear Ct. CT17: Dover 6A 28

King Lear's Way CT17: Dover 6B 28
Kingly Way CT17: Dover 4A 28
King's Av. TN23: Ashf 3E 35
Kingsbridge Ct. CT20: F'stone 3H 5
Kings Chase TN24: W'boro 3C 36
King's Cl. CT14: Kgdn 2G 13
Kings Ct. CT14: Walm 2H 11
(off King St.)
KINGSDOWN .2H 13
Kingsdown Hill CT14: Kgdn 2G 13
Kingsdown Holiday Camp CT14: Kgdn . .2H 13
Kingsdown Rd. CT14: Kgdn, Walm 3H 11
CT15: St Marg 3D 18
Kingsford Cl. CT16: Dover 2G 41
Kingsford Ct. CT17: Dover 1A 6 (2B 28)
Kingsford St. TN25: Mers 1F 41
Kingsford Ter. TN23: Ashf 1E 39
King's Head La. CT21: Hythe 5E 57
Kingsland Cotts. TN25: Westw 3D 30
Kingsland Gdns. CT14: Walm 5F 11
Kingsland La. TN25: Westw . . . .4C 30 & 1E 31
Kingsmead CT19: F'stone 5H 49
Kings Mdw. TN25: Kenn 4A 32
KINGSNORTH .3F 39
Kingsnorth Ct. CT20: F'stone 2H 59
Kingsnorth Gdns. CT20: F'stone 2H 59
Kingsnorth Ind. Est. TN23: Ashf 6F 35
Kingsnorth Rd. TN23: Ashf 2E 39
Kings Pde. TN24: Kenn 3B 4
Kings Prospect TN24: W'boro 1A 40
Kings Rd. CT17: Dover 4A 28
CT20: F'stone 1D 58
Kings Ropewalk CT17: Dover 6B 28
Kingston Cl. CT17: Dover 6H 15
Kingstone Ct. CT20: F'stone 3H 59
King St. CT14: Deal 5H 9
CT14: Walm 2H 11
CT16: Dover 5E 7 (4D 28)
Kingswood TN24: Kenn 6H 31
Kingswood Vs. CT17: Dover 1A 28
Kinneys La. TN24: Kenn 1H 35
Kinson Way CT16: Whitf 4A 16
Kipling Rd. TN23: Ashf 3A 4 (3F 35)
Kipping Cl. CT18: H'nge 1G 49
Kirk Gdns. CT14: Walm 3F 11
Kirk Vw. TN23: Ashf 5A 34
Kirton Cl. CT18: H'nge 1F 49
Kitchener Rd. CT17: Dover 4A 28
Kitchener Sq. CT19: F'stone 5C 50
Kither Rd. TN23: Ashf 6E 35
Knatchbull Way TN25: Bra L 2E 43
Knights Rd. CT16: Dover 3G 7 (3E 29)
Knights Templar Church (remains of) 5C 28
(off Citadel Rd.)
Knights Templars CT17: Dover 5C 28
Knights Way CT16: Dover 6A 16
Knock Rd. TN23: Ashf 6E 35
Knockwood Rd. TN30: Tent 4C 64
(not continuous)
Knoll Ct. CT15: St Marg 3D 18
CT20: F'stone 5E 5 (3A 60)
Knoll La. TN23: Ashf 6B 34
Knoll Pl. CT14: Walm 4G 11
Knott Cres. TN24: W'boro 6C 36
Knotts La. CT15: St Marg 3D 18
Knotts Sq. TN23: Ashf 3C 34
Kohima Pl. CT15: Gus 1F 29
Kowlam Pl. CT15: Gus 6F 17

L

Laburnum Cl. CT16: Dover 5G 15
Lachlan Way CT20: S'gte 4F 59
Lacton Oast TN24: W'boro 5C 36
Lacton Way TN24: W'boro 5C 36
Ladies Wlk. CT21: Hythe 5E 57
Lady Garne Rd. CT15: W Hou 6B 26
Ladywell CT16: Dover 3D 6 (3D 28)
Ladywell Ho. CT16: Dover 3D 6
Lakemead TN23: Ashf 5C 34
Lamberhurst M. TN23: Ashf 1C 38
Lambert Ho. CT14: Deal 2F 11
Lambton Rd. CT17: Dover 2A 28
Lancaster Av. CT18: Cap F 3F 51
Lancaster Ho. CT14: Deal 6E 9
CT17: Dover 4D 6
Lancaster Rd. CT17: Dover 5D 6 (4D 28)
Lancaster Way TN23: Ashf 1D 34

Lancelot Cl. CT14: Deal 2E 11
Landbury Wlk. TN25: Ashf 1D 34
Lane, The CT15: Gus 3E 17
Lanfranc Rd. CT14: Deal 3G 9
Langdale TN23: Ashf 4C 34
Langdon Cliffs Viewpoint 2H 29
Langdon Cl. CT15: St Marg 4D 18
Langdon Rd. CT19: F'stone 6D 48
Langholm Rd. TN23: Ashf 6E 35
(not continuous)
Langhorne Gdns. CT20: F'stone 6E 5
Langney Dr. TN23: Ashf 1B 38
Langton Ct. CT14: Deal 3G 9
Lapwing Cl. CT18: H'nge 2G 49
Lapwing Dr. TN23: Kgnt 2D 38
Larch Wlk. TN24: Kenn 5G 31
Lascelles Rd. CT17: Dover 5A 28
Latchgate CT20: S'gte 4C 58
La-Tene CT14: Deal 3F 11
Lathe Barn 4B 62
Laurel Cl. CT20: F'stone 1E 59
Laurel Ct. CT17: Dover 6E 49
Laurence Hamilton La. TN23: Ashf 2C 34
Laurens Van Der Post Way TN23: Ashf . . .2C 34
Laureston Pl. CT16: Dover 3F 7 (3E 29)
Lawn Rd. CT14: Walm 4G 11
Lawrence Cl. CT19: F'stone 1F 59
Lawrence Ct. CT19: F'stone 1H 5 (1C 60)
TN24: W'boro 1A 40
Lea Cl. CT21: Hythe 3D 56
Leacon Rd. TN23: Ashf 4C 34
Leafield TN25: S'ndge 4B 44
Leahurst Ct. CT14: Deal 5G 15
Leander Ct. CT14: Deal 2E 11
Leas, The CT14: Deal 3H 13
CT20: F'stone 6E 5 (4G 59)
(not continuous)
Leas Cliff Hall 6E 5 (3A 60)
Leaside Cotts. CT21: Hythe 4D 56
Leas Lift, The 6G 5 (3B 60)
Leas Rd. CT14: Deal 1F 11
Leaveland Cl. TN23: Ashf 1D 38
Lees, The TN25: Bou L 1A 32
Lees Close, The TN25: Bra L 2D 42
Lees Rd. TN24: W'boro 4C 36
(not continuous)
TN25: Bra L, E Bra 2D 42
Leeswood TN24: W'boro 4D 36
Leighton Ct. CT17: Dover 1B 6 (2C 28)
Leighton Rd. CT16: Dover 1B 6 (2C 28)
Leivers Rd. CT14: Deal 2E 11
Lenacre Av. CT16: Whitf 2H 15
Lenacre La. CT16: Whitf 2H 15
Lenacre St. TN25: E'well 1E 31
Lennard Ct. CT20: F'stone 3H 5
Lennard Rd. CT20: F'stone 3H 5 (2C 60)
Le Roux Cl. CT18: H'nge 1F 49
Lesley Chalk Ho. TN23: Ashf 4C 4 (3G 35)
Leslie Cres. TN30: St Mic 3B 64
Leslie Glibert La. TN23: Ashf 2C 34
Lewis Cl. TN23: Ashf 6D 34
Lewisham Rd. CT17: Dover 6G 15
Lewis Rd. CT18: H'nge 2F 49
Leyburne Rd. CT16: Dover 2E 7 (2D 28)
LICKPOT HILL 3H 21
Lighthouse Rd. CT15: St Marg 5D 18
Lilac Ct. TN23: Ashf 5D 34
LILYVALE 3F 43
Lilyvale Cotts. TN25: Sme 3F 43
Lilyvale Rd. TN25: Sme 3F 43
Lime Cl. CT14: Deal 3F 11
Lime Ct. TN24: Kenn 4H 31
Limekiln Rdbt. CT17: Dover 5D 28
Limekiln St. CT17: Dover 6D 28
Limes, The TN23: Kgnt 2E 39
Limes Cl. TN30: Tent 5C 64
Limes Rd. CT16: Dover 1C 6 (2C 28)
CT19: F'stone 1F 59
Lime Vs. CT4: Elham 1H 21
Linces, The CT16: Dover 6B 16
Linden Cres. CT19: F'stone 1G 5 (1B 60)
Linden Dr. CT4: Elham 2H 21
Linden Rd. TN24: Ashf 3H 35
Lindens CT21: Hythe 5E 57
Lindens, The TN30: Tent 4B 64
Link, The TN23: Ashf 6C 34
Link Park, The CT21: Lymp 3C 54
Links Ct. CT14: Deal 2G 9
Links Rd. CT14: Deal 3G 9

Linksway CT19: F'stone 6G 49
Linksway Cl. CT19: F'stone 6H 49
Lister Cl. CT14: Deal 6G 9
CT17: Dover 1A 6 (2B 28)
Lister Way CT20: S'gte 4F 59
Little Av. CT14: Deal 2D 10
Littlebrook Cl. TN23: Ashf 2E 35
Lit. Brook Rd. TN23: Ashf 2E 35
Lit. Burton Cen. TN24: Kenn 1A 36
(off Richmond Meech Dr.)
Little Chequers TN25: Wye 1G 33
Little Hempen TN23: Ashf 5B 34
Little Hill TN30: St Mic 3B 64
Little Knoll TN23: Ashf 5D 34
Little Mead CT19: F'stone 6G 49
Little Redbrooks CT21: Hythe 4B 56
Little Satmar Holiday Pk. CT18: Cap F . . .2H 51
Little Switzerland Caravan & Camping Site
. . . . .5E 51
Liverpool Rd. CT14: Walm 2H 11
Livingstone Cl. TN29: Dym 5F 63
Lloyd Ct. CT14: Deal 4H 9
(off High St.)
Lockeringe La. CT15: Alk 3D 24
Lockholt Cl. TN23: Ashf 2C 34
Lodge Wood Dr. TN25: Ashf 6C 30
London Beach Golf Course 1A 64
London Pl. CT20: F'stone 3H 5
London Rd. CT14: Deal, Shol 6D 8
CT16: Dover, Temp E 3D 14
CT17: Dover 1A 6 (1B 28)
(Lorne Rd.)
CT17: Dover 5G 15
(Whitfield Hill)
CT21: Hythe 4A 56
London St. CT20: F'stone 3H 5 (2C 60)
Lonefield TN26: Shad 5D 38
Longacre Rd. TN23: Ashf 6B 34
Longage Hill CT4: R Min 1C 20
CT18: Lym'ge 1C 20
Long Barrow, The TN24: Ashf 1A 40
Long Beech TN23: Ashf 4C 34
Longbridge TN24: W'boro 4D 36
Longbridge Ter. CT21: Hythe 6B 56
Longfield TN30: Tent 6A 64
Longfield Rd. CT17: Dover 6A 6 (5B 28)
Longford Ter. CT20: F'stone 5F 5 (3B 60)
Longford Way CT20: F'stone 6F 5 (3B 60)
Long Length TN23: Kgnt 4B 38
TN26: Kgnt 4B 38
Longport Rd. CT18: F'stone 6B 48
Long Row TN25: Mers 5F 41
Long's Acre TN25: Wye 2G 33
Lonsdale Ct. CT16: Dover 2D 6
Lookers La. CT21: Hythe 4D 56
Lord Cornwalls Ct. CT19: F'stone 5A 50
Lord Roberts Av. CT14: Walm 3H 11
Lord Warden Av. CT14: Walm 3H 11
Lord Warden Sq. CT17: Dover 6D 28
Lorne Rd. CT16: Dover 1A 6 (1B 28)
Lorraine Ct. CT19: F'stone 1H 5
Loudon Cl. TN23: Ashf 2C 34
Loudon Path TN23: Ashf 2C 34
Loudon Way TN23: Ashf 2C 34
Loughborough La. CT18: Lym'ge 6A 20
Lourdes Mnr. Cl. TN25: S'ndge 4B 44
Lwr. Blackhouse Hill CT21: Hythe 5F 57
Lower Corniche CT21: S'gte, Hythe 5C 58
Lwr. Denmark Rd. TN23: Ashf 5G 35
Lwr. Hayesbank TN24: Ashf 2C 4 (2G 35)
Lwr. Mill La. CT14: Deal 6G 9
Lower Pemberton TN25: Ashf 4F 31
Lwr. Queens Rd. TN24: Ashf 2C 4 (2G 35)
Lower Rd. CT16: Temp E 4F 15
CT17: Dover 5F 15
Lower Rd. E. CT16: Dover 3H 29
Lower Rd. W. CT16: Dover 3G 29
Lwr. Sandgate Rd. CT20: F'stone . .6E 5 (4H 59)
(not continuous)
Lwr. Vicarage Rd. TN24: Kenn 4G 31
Lwr. Wall Rd. CT15: W Hyt 1A 62
LOWER WALMER 2G 11
Lowslip Hill CT15: W Hou 6B 26
Lowther Rd. CT17: Dover 3A 6 (3B 28)
Loxwood Cl. CT16: Whitf 2B 16
Lucerne La. CT15: Mart, Mart M 4A 12
Lucilla Av. TN23: Kgnt 3D 38
Luckhurst Rd. CT17: Dover 6G 15
TN24: W'boro 6C 36
Lucknow Cl. CT15: Gus 6F 17

Lucy Av. CT19: F'stone 6G *49*
Lucy's Av. CT21: Hythe 5F *57*
Lucys Hill CT21: Hythe 5D *56*
Luddenham Cl. TN23: Ashf 1D *38*
Lukes Cl. CT17: Dover 2B *28*
Lukin Ho. CT21: Hythe 6B *56*
LYDDEN 2A *14*
Lydden Hill CT15: Lyd'n 1A *14*
Lydden Temple Ewell National Nature Reserve
. . . . .2D *14*
Lydia Rd. CT14: Walm 3E *11*
Lyell Cl. CT21: Hythe 6C *56*
LYMINGE 5E *21*
LYMPNE 4E *55*
Lympne Hill CT21: Lymp 5E *55*
Lympne Ind. Est. CT21: Lymp 4C *54*
Lympne Pl. Cotts. CT21: Lymp 5C *54*
Lyndhurst Rd. CT17: Dover 1G *27*
Lyndon Way CT18: Lym'ge 4E *21*
Lynsted Cl. TN23: Ashf 1D *38*
Lynton Rd. CT21: Hythe 6E *57*
Lynwood CT19: F'stone 6H *49*
Lysander Wlk. CT18: H'nge 1G *49*

M

Mabledon Av. TN24: Ashf 4H *35*
Macdonald Rd. CT17: Dover 2A *28*
Mace Ind. Est. TN24: Ashf 2D *4* (2G *35*)
Mace La. TN24: Ashf 3D *4* (3G *35*)
MacFarlane's World of Butterflies 1H *23*
Mackenzie Dr. CT20: F'stone 2D *58*
Mackenzie Ter. *CT16: Dover* *6B 16*
(off Selkirk Rd.)
Mackeson Ct. *CT21: Hythe* *5D 56*
(off Military Rd.)
Madeira Ct. CT20: F'stone 4H *59*
Magazine Rd. TN24: Ashf 2A *4* (2F *35*)
Magdala Rd. CT17: Dover 1A *6* (2B *28*)
Magistrates' Court
Dover 4E *7* (3D *28*)
Folkestone 3A *60*
Magness Rd. CT14: Deal 3E *11*
Magpie Hall Rd. TN26: Stu X 4B *38*
Magpie La. CT4: R Min 1D *20*
Magpie Lodge *CT16: Dover* *1B 28*
(off Mayfield Av.)
Maidstone Rd. TN24: Ashf 2A *4* (1H *35*)
TN25: Ashf .4A *30*
TN26: Hoth 4A *30*
Maine Cl. CT16: Dover 6B *16*
Main Rd. TN25: S'ndge 6H *43*
Maison Dieu Gdns. CT16: Dover . . .3E *7* (3D *28*)
Maison Dieu Pl. CT16: Dover 3D *6* (3D *28*)
Maison Dieu Rd. CT16: Dover 2D *6* (2D *28*)
Majestic Pde. CT20: F'stone 6E *5* (3A *60*)
Malcolm Sargent Rd. TN23: Ashf 1F *39*
Mallards TN24: W'boro 6H *35*
Malmains Rd. CT17: Dover 4A *28*
Malthouse Hill CT21: Hythe 5D *56*
Malt Ho. La. TN30: Tent 6A *64*
Maltings, The CT14: Walm 5F *11*
CT21: Hythe *5D 56*
(off High St.)
Malvern Cotts. CT16: Dover 5G *15*
Malvern Mdw. CT16: Temp E 4G *15*
Malvern Rd. CT16: Temp E 4G *15*
CT17: Dover 5B *6* (4C *28*)
TN24: Ashf 1B *4* (1F *35*)
Manger's La. CT16: Dover 1A *28*
Mangers Pl. CT16: Dover 6A *16*
Manitoba Ho. *CT16: Dover* *6C 16*
(off Winnipeg Cl.)
Manley Cl. CT16: Whitf 2A *16*
Mannering Cl. CT17: Dover 6H *15*
Manor Av. CT14: Deal 1F *11*
Manor Cl. CT14: Deal 1E *11*
Mnr. Farm Cl. CT21: Lymp 3E *55*
Manorfield TN23: Ashf 5C *34*
Manor Gdns. CT16: Whitf 1A *16*
Manor Ho. Dr. TN23: Kgnt 3G *39*
Manor Ho. La. CT18: Cap F 6H *25*
Manor Leaze TN25: Sme 2F *43*
Manor M. CT14: R'wld 2D *12*
Manor Ri. CT17: Dover 5A *28*
Manor Rd. CT14: Deal 1E *11*
CT17: Dover .5A *28*
CT20: F'stone 4E *5* (3A *60*)

Manor Row *TN30: Tent* *6A 64*
(off High St.)
Manor Way CT20: F'stone 3A *60*
TN23: Ashf 1D *34*
(not continuous)
Manse Fld. TN25: Bra L 2E *43*
Mansion Gdns. CT16: Whitf 5A *16*
Mantles Hill CT14: Ripp 4B *10*
Maple Cl. TN23: Ashf 3C *34*
Maple Dr. CT18: H'nge 6A *24*
Maplefield Gdns. CT18: H'nge 6A *24*
Mardol Rd. TN24: Kenn 6G *31*
Maresfield Cl. CT16: Dover 1B *28*
Margaret St. CT20: F'stone 4H *5* (2C *60*)
Marina, The CT14: Deal 2H *9*
Marina Ct. CT14: Deal 3H *9*
Marine Av. TN29: Dym 6D *62*
Marine Ct. CT16: Dover 5G *7* (4E *29*)
Marine Cres. CT14: Deal 6G *5* (3B *60*)
Marine Pde. CT16: Dover 5F *7* (4E *29*)
(not continuous)
CT20: F'stone 6G *5* (3B *60*)
CT21: Hythe .6E *57*
Marine Pde. M. CT20: F'stone 5H *5* (3C *60*)
Marine Point CT20: F'stone 4H *59*
Marine Prom. CT20: F'stone 3B *60*
Marine Rd. CT14: Walm 4F *11*
Marine Ter. CT20: F'stone 5H *5* (3C *60*)
Marine Wlk. CT20: F'stone 6E *5* (4H *59*)
Marine Wlk. St. CT21: Hythe 5E *57*
Marjan Cl. CT17: Dover 2A *28*
Market Hill CT21: Hythe 5E *57*
Market La. TN23: Ashf 4B *4*
Market Pl. CT20: F'stone 4G *5* (2B *60*)
Market Sq. CT16: Dover 5E *7* (4D *28*)
Market St. CT14: Deal 5H *9*
Markland Rd. CT17: Dover 4H *27*
Marlborough Ct. CT20: F'stone 3H *59*
CT21: Hythe .6F *57*
Marlborough Rd. CT14: Deal 3E *11*
CT17: Dover .4H *27*
Marlborough Way TN24: Kenn 4B *32*
Marler Rd. CT19: F'stone 1E *59*
Marlowe Rd. CT16: Dover 6B *16*
TN23: Ashf 3A *4* (3F *35*)
Marmion Way TN23: Ashf 5A *34*
Marre La. CT18: H'nge 2F *49*
Marshalls Land TN30: St Mic 2A *64*
Marshall St. CT19: F'stone 1G *5* (6B *50*)
Marsh La. CT14: Deal, Shol 5D *8*
Marsh Vw. CT21: Hythe 1G *63*
Martello Cotts. CT21: Hythe 6B *56*
Martello Ct. CT20: F'stone 3H *5*
Martello Dr. CT21: Hythe 6B *56*
Martello Ind. Est. CT19: F'stone 1D *60*
Martello Rd. CT20: F'stone 2H *5* (1C *60*)
(Dover Rd.)
CT20: F'stone 4D *58*
(West Rd.)
Martello Ter. CT20: S'gte 4F *59*
Marten Rd. CT20: F'stone 4H *59*
Martha Cl. CT19: F'stone 6H *49*
MARTIN 5A *12*
Martin Dale Cres. CT15: Mart M 5A *12*
Martin Ho. TN25: Wye 2G *33*
MARTIN MILL 5A *12*
Martin Mill Station (Rail) 5A *12*
Martins Cl. TN30: Tent 5C *64*
Martin's Way CT21: Hythe 1H *63*
Mary Ann Cotts. *CT19: F'stone* *6E 49*
(off Ashley Av.)
Maryland Ct. CT21: Hythe 4F *57*
Mary Rd. CT14: Deal 2E *11*
Masons Rd. CT17: Dover 2B *28*
Matfield Cl. TN23: Ashf 1E *39*
Mathon Ct. TN24: Kenn 6G *31*
Matthews Cl. CT14: Deal 5G *9*
Matthew's Pl. CT16: Dover 2C *6* (2C *28*)
Maunsell Pl. TN24: Ashf 6H *35*
Maurice Buckmaster La.
TN23: Ashf 2C *34*
MAXTON 5A *28*
Maxton Cl. CT17: Dover 5A *28*
Maxton Rd. CT17: Dover 5A *28*
Maxwell Pl. CT14: Deal 1G *11*
Mayers Rd. CT14: Walm 4E *11*
Mayfield Av. CT16: Dover 1B *28*
Mayfield Cl. CT16: Dover 1B *28*
Mayfield Gdns. CT16: Dover 1C *28*

Mayfield Rd. CT16: Whitf 3A *16*
CT18: Lym'ge 5E *21*
Mayfly Dr. CT18: H'nge 1G *49*
Mayhew Cl. TN23: Ashf 5E *35*
Mayor's Pl. *TN30: Tent* *6A 64*
(off Woodbury Gdns.)
Maypits TN23: Ashf 5D *34*
Maypole Cl. CT18: H'nge 5H *23*
Maypole Gro. CT18: H'nge 5H *23*
May Tree Cotts. CT14: Ripp 5B *10*
Maytree Cotts. TN24: Svgtn 2D *40*
Meade, The CT18: H'nge 1F *49*
Meadowbrook CT20: S'gte 3E *59*
Meadowbrook Cl. TN24: Kenn 5H *31*
Meadowbrook Ct. CT20: S'gte 3E *59*
Meadowbrook Rd. TN24: Kenn 5H *31*
Meadow Cl. CT18: H'nge 1H *49*
Meadow Gro. TN25: S'ndge 5B *44*
Meadow Rd. TN23: Ashf 1E *35*
Meadowsweet Ho. TN23: Ashf 4E *35*
Meadow Vw. TN26: Hoth 2C *30*
Meadow Way CT21: Hythe 1H *63*
Mead Rd. CT19: F'stone 1F *5* (1B *60*)
TN24: W'boro 6A *36*
Mead Wlk. TN23: Ashf 5C *34*
Meadway CT17: Dover 6F *15*
Meggett La. CT15: Alk 3F *25*
Megone Cl. CT18: H'nge 1G *49*
Melbourne Av. CT16: Dover 6B *16*
CT16: Dover, Whitf 4B *16*
Melcombe Cl. TN23: Ashf 6A *34*
Memorial M. CT18: H'nge 1F *49*
Mendip TN24: Ashf 1A *4* (1F *35*)
Menzies Av. CT14: Walm 4F *11*
Menzies Rd. CT16: Whitf 5H *15*
Merchants Pl. CT20: F'stone 4G *5*
Meriden Wlk. *CT18: Etch'l* *2F 47*
(off St Mary's Dr.)
Meridian Ct. TN23: Ashf 5C *34*
Meridian Ho. TN23: Ashf 4A *4*
Merino Way TN23: Kgnt 2C *38*
Merlin Way TN23: Ashf 6C *34*
MERSHAM 3G *41*
Meryl Gdns. CT14: Walm 4F *11*
Metropole, The CT17: Dover 5E *7*
Metropole Ct. CT20: F'stone 4H *59*
Metropole Galleries, The 4H *59*
Metropole Rd. E. CT20: F'stone 4H *59*
Metropole Rd. W. CT20: F'stone 4H *59*
Middelburg Ho. CT19: F'stone 1D *58*
Middelburg Sq. CT20: F'stone 5F *5* (3B *60*)
Middle Cl. TN23: Gt Cha 4A *34*
MIDDLE DEAL 5G *9*
Middle Deal Rd. CT14: Deal 6E *9*
Middle Mead CT19: F'stone 6H *49*
Middle Row TN24: Ashf 3C *4*
Middle St. CT14: Deal 4H *9*
(not continuous)
TN23: Ashf 4B *4* (3F *35*)
Middleton Cl. CT14: Walm 1G *11*
Midsummer Hill TN24: Kenn 5H *31*
Mildred Cotts. CT19: F'stone 6F *49*
Milestone Cl. CT19: F'stone 6G *49*
Milestone Rd. CT14: Deal 6F *9*
Military Rd. CT17: Dover 5D *6* (4D *28*)
CT20: F'stone, S'gte 2D *58*
CT21: Hythe .5C *56*
Millais Rd. CT16: Dover 1B *6* (2C *28*)
Millbank Rd. TN23: Kgnt 2D *38*
(not continuous)
Mill Bay CT20: F'stone 4G *5* (2B *60*)
Millbrook CT21: Hythe 4F *57*
Millbrook Mdw. TN23: Ashf 4C *34*
Mill Bus. Park, The TN26: Hoth 4B *30*
Mill Cl. CT17: Dover 1H *27*
Mill Cotts. CT16: Temp E 4F *15*
Mill Ct. TN24: Ashf 3H *35*
Milldale Cl. CT14: Deal 1F *11*
Miller Cl. CT14: Deal 3G *9*
TN24: Ashf 3H *35*
Miller Cotts. TN24: Ashf 3H *35*
Millers Cl. TN25: Stanf 5F *45*
Millfield CT15: St Marg 2D *18*
CT18: H'nge .6A *24*
CT20: F'stone 5E *5* (3A *60*)
TN23: Ashf 4B *34*
Millfield Cl. CT18: H'nge 6H *23*
Mill Flds. Rd. CT21: Hythe 5B *56*

MILL HILL 2E 11
Mill Hill CT14: Deal 2E 11
Millhill CT4: O'nge 1F 21
Mill Hill Ct. CT14: Deal 2F 11
Mill Ho. CT17: Dover 6H 15
Mill La. CT15: W Hou 6B 26
    CT16: Dover 5F 7 (4E 29)
    CT16: Whitf 1A 16
    CT18: H'nge 1H 49
    CT21: Hythe 4F 57
    TN24: W'boro 4C 36
    TN25: Kenn 4C 32
    TN30: Tent 4B 64
Millmeade Ct. CT20: F'stone 4E 5 (2A 60)
Mill M. CT14: Deal 1F 11
Mill Race CT17: Dover 6H 15
Mill Rd. CT14: Deal 1F 11
    CT21: Hythe 5F 57
Millstream Grn. TN24: W'boro 6B 36
Mill St. CT16: Temp E 4F 15
Mill Vw. TN24: W'boro 5B 36
Milne Rd. TN24: W'boro 5B 16
Milton Cl. CT16: Dover 5B 16
Milton Rd. CT16: Dover 6H 15
    TN23: Ashf 3A 4 (3F 35)
Minerva Av. CT16: Dover 1C 28
Minnis La. CT15: Dover 2D 26
    CT17: Dover 2D 26
Minnis Ter. CT17: Dover 1A 28
Minter Av. CT18: D'sole 4F 23
Minter Cl. CT18: D'sole 4F 23
Minters Ind. Est. CT14: Deal 5G 9
Missenden Ct. CT20: F'stone 3G 5
Mitchell Av. CT18: H'nge 6H 23
Mitchell St. CT19: F'stone 1D 58
Moat Farm Cl. CT19: F'stone 6A 50
Moat Farm Rd.
    CT19: F'stone 1E 5 (6A 50)
Moat Fld. Mdw. TN23: Kgnt 3F 39
Moat's Bulwark 4H 7 (3E 29)
Moat Way TN24: Ashf 1B 40
Mockford All. TN30: Tent 6A 64
    (off High St.)
Mock La. TN23: Gt Cha 1A 38
Molloy Rd. TN26: Shad 5D 38
Monastery Av. CT16: Dover 2E 7 (2D 28)
Mongeham Chu. Cl. CT14: Gt Mon 2B 10
Mongeham Rd.
    CT14: Gt Mon, Ripp, Shol 4B 10
Monins Rd. CT17: Dover 4B 28
MONKS HORTON 1F 45
Monks Way CT16: Dover 6A 16
Monkton Cl. TN23: Ashf 1D 38
Montacue Ct. CT20: F'stone 3H 59
Montcalm Ter. CT16: Dover 6C 16
    (off Winnipeg Cl.)
Montfort Cl. TN23: Ashf 6D 34
Montgomery Way CT19: F'stone 5B 50
Montpelier Bus. Pk. TN23: Ashf 4D 34
Montreal Cl. CT16: Dover 6B 16
Monument Way TN24: Ashf 1A 40
MOORSTOCK 3A 44
Moorstock La. TN25: M Hor, S'ndge 6A 44
MOREHALL 1F 59
Morehall Av. CT19: F'stone 1F 59
Moreton Ter. TN26: Shad 5C 38
Morgan Cl. TN24: W'boro 5B 36
Morrison Rd. CT20: F'stone 2H 5 (1C 60)
Mortimer Cl. TN23: Ashf 6F 35
Mortimer Rd. CT16: Dover 3H 7 (3F 29)
Mountbatten Way TN25: Bra L 1E 43
Mt. Pleasant CT17: Dover 5D 6
    TN30: Tent 5C 64
Mt. Pleasant Cl. CT18: Lym'ge 4E 21
Mt. Pleasant Rd. CT20: F'stone . . .3G 5 (2B 60)
Mount Rd. CT17: Dover 6A 28
Mounts Cl. CT14: Deal 6E 9
Mount St. CT21: Hythe 5E 57
Mount Vw. TN25: Ashf 1D 34
Moyle Cl. CT21: Hythe 6E 57
Moyle Twr. Rd. CT21: Hythe 6E 57
Mudie Cl. CT18: H'nge 6G 23
Mulberry Cl. CT21: Hythe 4F 57
Mulberry Gdns. TN30: Tent 5B 64
Mulberry Rd. TN23: Ashf 2B 34
Muscovy Rd. TN25: Kenn 3G 31
Musgrove TN23: Ashf 6A 4 (5E 35)
Myrtle Ct. TN23: Kgnt 4E 39
Myrtle Grn. TN23: Ashf 1B 34

Myrtle Gro. TN23: Ashf 6C 34
Myrtle Rd. CT19: F'stone 1H 5 (1C 60)

N

NACCOLT .5G 33
Naccolt Cotts. TN25: Brook 6G 33
Naccolt Rd. TN25: Brook, Hin 5G 33
Nailbourne Ct. CT18: Lym'ge 4E 21
Naildown Cl. CT21: Hythe 4A 58
Naildown Rd. CT21: Hythe 4A 58
Nairne Cl. TN26: Shad 6C 38
Namur Pl. CT15: Gus 6F 17
Napchester Rd. CT15: Whitf 1A 16
    CT16: Whitf 1A 16
Napier Gdns. CT21: Hythe 6E 57
Napier Rd. CT16: Dover 6B 16
Narrabeen Rd. CT19: F'stone 1E 59
Naseby Av. CT20: F'stone 2D 58
Nash Hill CT18: Lym'ge 5E 21
Natal Rd. CT16: Dover 5C 16
Nats La. TN25: Brook 1H 37
Neason Ct. CT19: F'stone 1D 60
Neason Way CT19: F'stone 1D 60
Nelson Cl. TN24: W'boro 5D 36
NELSON PARK 1D 18
Nelson Pk. Rd. CT15: St Marg 1C 18
Nelson St. CT14: Deal 4H 9
Nelson Ter. CT16: Dover 6B 16
    (off Alberta Cl.)
Neptune Ct. CT14: Walm 1H 11
    (off Trafalgar Rd.)
Nettlefield TN24: Kenn 6A 32
Neville M. CT14: Deal 6H 9
Nevill Gdns. CT14: Walm 4F 11
NEWBARN .1D 46
New Beach Holiday Pk. TN29: Dym 5E 63
New Bridge CT16: Dover 6F 7 (4E 29)
Newbury Cl. CT17: Dover 4H 27
    CT20: F'stone 2D 58
Newcastle La. CT15: Ewe M 6A 14
New Dover Rd. CT18: Cap F 5E 51
Newenden Cl. TN23: Ashf 1C 38
NEWINGREEN 2E 55
NEWINGTON 6A 48
Newington Mdw. CT21: Hythe 4F 57
Newington Rd. CT18: N'tn 6A 48
    CT18: N'tn, Peene 5A 48
Newlands CT16: Whitf 2B 16
    TN23: Ashf 1B 38
Newlands Dr. CT14: Walm 5F 11
New Lincoln Ho's. CT19: F'stone 5B 50
Newlyns Mdw. CT15: Alk 2H 25
Newman Cl. CT21: Hythe 6D 56
Newmans Cl. CT21: Hythe 6D 56
New Rectory La. TN23: Kgnt 3F 39
New Rents TN23: Ashf 3B 4 (3F 35)
New Rd. CT21: Elham 2H 21
    CT21: Hythe 6D 56
    CT21: Salt 3D 56
New St. CT14: Deal 4H 9
    CT17: Dover 5E 7 (4D 28)
    CT20: F'stone 3G 5 (2B 60)
    TN24: Ashf 2A 4 (3F 35)
    (not continuous)
NEW TOWN 5H 35
New Town Grn. TN24: Ashf 5H 35
Newtown Rd. TN23: Ashf 6D 4 (4G 35)
    TN24: Ashf 5H 35
NHS WALK-IN CENTRE (FOLKESTONE) . .2E 5
    (within Royal Victoria Hospital)
Niagara Ho. CT16: Dover 6B 16
    (off Toronto Cl.)
Nicholas Rd. TN25: Ashf 4E 31
Nightingale Av. CT21: Hythe 1H 63
Nightingale Cl. TN24: Svgtn 6C 36
Nightingale Rd. CT16: Dover 1B 6 (1C 28)
Nine Acres TN24: Kenn 6G 31
Ninn Cotts. TN23: Gt Cha 4A 34
Ninn La. TN23: Gt Cha 3A 34
Noah's Ark Rd. CT17: Dover 3A 6 (3A 28)
Noah's Ark Ter. CT17: Dover 3A 6 (3B 28)
Noakes Mdw. TN23: Ashf 5D 34
Norfolk Dr. TN23: Ashf 3E 35
Normandy Way TN23: Ashf 6B 34
Norman Rd. CT15: St Marg 3F 19
    TN23: Ashf 6F 35
Norman St. CT17: Dover 4D 6 (3D 28)

Norman Tailyour Ho. CT14: Deal 6H 9
    (off Hope Rd.)
Norrington Mead CT19: F'stone 6G 49
Nth. Barrack Rd. CT14: Walm 1H 11
Nth. Barracks CT14: Deal 1G 11
Northbourne Av. CT17: Dover 3A 6 (3B 28)
Northbourne Rd. CT14: Gt Mon, N'bne . . .1A 10
Northbrooke TN24: Ashf 1C 4 (2G 35)
Northbrooke La. TN24: Ashf 1D 4 (2G 35)
Nth. Camber Way CT16: Dover 2H 29
North Cl. CT20: F'stone 3D 58
North Cl. Bus. Pk. CT20: F'stone 3D 58
Northcote Rd. CT14: Deal 6H 9
    CT14: Kgdn 3H 13
North Ct. CT14: Deal 4G 9
Northdown TN24: Ashf 1G 35
Nth. East Rd. CT16: Dover 3H 29
Northfall Rd. CT15: Alk 2H 25
North La. CT20: S'gte 4E 59
North Lea CT14: Deal 4G 9
NORTH LYMINGE 4E 21
Nth. Lyminge La. CT18: Lym'ge 4E 21
Nth. Military Rd. CT17: Dover 6C 6 (4C 28)
North Pends TN24: Kenn 5A 32
North Promenade CT14: Deal 4H 9
North Rd. CT14: Kgdn 1H 13
    CT17: Dover 4B 6 (3C 28)
    CT20: F'stone 3C 58
    CT21: Hythe 4C 56
North Rd. W. CT21: Hythe 4C 56
North St. CT14: Deal 4H 9
    CT17: Dover 6A 6 (4B 28)
    CT19: F'stone 4H 5 (2C 60)
    TN24: Ashf 3C 4 (3G 35)
    (not continuous)
Northumberland Av. TN24: Kenn 6H 31
Northwall Ct. CT14: Deal 4G 9
Northwall M. CT14: Deal 4G 9
Northwall Rd. CT14: Deal 3E 9
Norway Drove CT15: St Marg 6E 13
Norwood Gdns. TN23: Ashf 3A 4 (3F 35)
Norwood St. TN23: Ashf 4B 4 (3F 35)
Nursery Cl. CT18: D'sole 4G 23
Nursery Flds. CT21: Hythe 5B 56
Nursery La. CT16: Whitf 2H 15
    CT18: D'sole 4G 23
Nutley Cl. TN24: Ashf 1D 4 (2G 35)

O

Oak Dr. CT18: H'nge 6H 23
Oakenpole TN23: Ashf 4C 34
Oakfield Rd. TN24: Kenn 6H 31
Oak Hall Pas. CT21: Hythe 5E 57
Oaklands TN23: Ashf 4D 34
    TN25: Mers 3G 41
Oaklands Cotts. CT21: Hythe 6A 56
Oakleigh Ho. TN23: Ashf 5C 34
Oaks, The CT18: H'nge 2H 49
Oaks Ga. TN30: Tent 5B 64
Oaks Rd. CT20: F'stone 1D 58
    TN30: Tent 5B 64
Oak St. CT14: Deal 5H 9
Oaks Vw. CT21: Hythe 1G 63
Oak Tree Rd. TN23: Ashf 5D 34
Oak Trees Bus. Pk. TN24: Ashf 1B 40
Oakvale Cl. CT17: Dover 4B 28
Oak Wlk. CT21: Hythe 5E 57
Oast Mdw. TN24: W'boro 4B 36
Occupation Rd. TN25: Wye 1H 33
Octavian Dr. CT21: Lymp 4E 55
Octavian Way TN23: Kgnt 2D 39
Odo Rd. CT17: Dover 3A 6 (3B 28)
Okehampton Cl. TN24: Kenn 4B 32
Olantigh Rd. TN25: Wye 1H 33
Old Ash Cl. TN24: Kenn 6G 31
Old Charlton Rd. CT16: Dover 1C 6 (1D 28)
Old Dover Rd. CT18: Cap F 4F 51
Old Flour Mill, The CT16: Dover 1A 6
Old Folkestone Rd.
    CT17: Dover . . . . .1H 53 & 6A 28
Old Gymnasium, The CT14: Walm 2G 11
OLD HAWKINGE 1C 50
Old High Street, The
    CT20: F'stone 4G 5 (2B 60)
Old Iron Foundry, The TN23: Ashf 3E 35

Old London Rd. CT21: Hythe 5A 56
Old Mead CT19: F'stone 6G 49
Old Mill M. CT19: F'stone 6E 49
Old Orchard TN23: Ashf 5B 34
OLD PARK 4A 16
Old Park Av. CT16: Dover 6A 16
Old Park Cl. CT16: Whitf 5A 16
Old Park Hill CT16: Dover 5A 16
Old Park Rd. CT16: Dover 1B 28
Old Pond Rd. TN23: Ashf 4D 34
Old Post Office M.
     CT21: Hythe 5D 56
Old Print Ho. CT16: Dover 4F 7
Old Railway Works TN24: Ashf 5H 35
Old Rectory, The TN25: Bou L 1A 32
Old Rectory Cl. CT18: H'nge 1H 49
     TN25: Mers .3G 41
Old Rd. CT4: Elham 2H 21
Old Roman Rd. CT15: Mart M 6A 12
Old Saltwood La. CT21: Salt 3D 56
Old School Ct. CT20: F'stone 3H 59
Old School M. CT20: S'gte 4F 59
                              (off Sandgate Hill)
Oldstairs Rd. CT14: Kgdn 5G 13
Old Tannery Cl. TN30: Tent 6A 64
Old Vicarage Gdns. TN25: Wye 1G 33
Ontario Way CT16: Dover 6B 16
Opie Wlk. CT18: H'nge 2F 49
Orbital Pk. TN24: Ashf 1B 40
                              (not continuous)
Orchard Av. CT14: Deal 6F 9
Orchard Caravan Pk. TN29: Burm 5B 62
Orchard Cl. CT16: Whitf 1H 15
     TN25: Mers 4G 41
Orchard Ct. TN23: Ashf 5F 35
Orchard Dr. CT17: Dover 6G 15
     CT21: Hythe .6D 56
     TN25: Wye 2H 33
Orchard Flds. CT21: Post 3A 46
Orchard Hgts. TN25: Ashf 6D 30
Orchard La. TN25: Kenn 5B 32
Orchard M. CT14: Deal 6H 9
Orchard Rd. TN30: St Mic 2A 64
Orchards, The CT4: Elham 2H 21
ORCHARD VALLEY .4C 56
Orchard Valley CT21: Hythe 5C 56
Orchard Vs. CT17: Dover 5G 15
Orchid Ct. TN23: Kgnt 5H 39
Orchids, The CT18: Etch'l 1F 47
     TN25: Mers 3G 41
Ordinance Way TN23: Ashf 1D 34
Orion Way TN24: W'boro 5A 36
Ormonde Ct. CT21: Hythe 6E 57
Ormonde Rd. CT20: F'stone 1C 60
     CT21: Hythe .6E 57
Orpins Cl. TN25: Bra L 1D 42
Orr Cl. CT18: H'nge 1F 49
Osborne Rd. CT14: Kgdn 1G 13
     TN24: W'boro 4A 36
Osier Fld. TN25: Kenn 4A 32
Osprey Ct. CT16: Dover 1B 28
     CT18: H'nge .2F 49
Oswald Pl. CT17: Dover 1B 28
Oswald Rd. CT17: Dover 1A 6 (1B 28)
Ottawa Cres. CT16: Dover 6C 16
Ottawa Way CT16: Dover 6C 16
                              (off Green La.)
Otterden Cl. TN23: Ashf 1D 34
                              (not continuous)
Otterpool La. CT21: Lymp 4B 54
     TN25: S'ndge 4B 54
OTTINGE 1F 21
Outdowns CT14: Deal 4G 9
Owen's Cl. CT21: Hythe 4B 58
Owen Sq. CT14: Walm 3F 11
Oxenden Rd. CT20: F'stone 3E 59
Oxen Lease TN23: Ashf 5C 34
Oxenturn Rd. TN25: Brook, Wye 4G 33
Oxford Ho. CT20: F'stone 3B 60
                              (off Oxford Ter.)
Oxford Ter. CT20: F'stone 5G 5 (3B 60)
Ox La. TN30: St Mic 3B 64

P

PADDLESWORTH .1C 48
Paddlesworth La. CT18: H'nge 1E 49
Paddock, The CT16: Dover 3E 7 (3D 28)

Paddock Cl. CT14: Shol 6D 8
     CT20: F'stone 2F 59
Paddock Rd. TN23: Ashf 6C 34
Paddocks, The CT18: D'sole 3G 23
     TN23: Gt Cha 4A 34
Padwell Cotts. TN23: Gt Cha 5A 34
Padwell La. TN23: Gt Cha 5A 34
Page Pl. CT19: F'stone 5B 50
Page Rd. CT18: H'nge 2F 49
Painesfield Cl. TN29: Burm 5A 62
PALMARSH 1H 63
Palmarsh Av. CT21: Hythe 1G 63
Palmarsh Cres. CT21: Hythe 1H 63
                              (Jubilee Cl.)
     CT21: Hythe .1H 63
                              (Palmarsh Av.)
Palmbeach Av. CT21: Hythe 1G 63
PALMER'S HILL 3A 50
Palmerston Av. CT14: Walm 2G 11
Palmerston Ct. CT14: Walm 3H 11
Palmerston Rd. CT16: Whitf 5H 15
Palmerston St. CT19: F'stone 2F 5 (1B 60)
Palm Tree Way CT18: Lym'ge 4D 20
Palting Way CT20: F'stone 4D 58
Pannell Dr. CT18: H'nge 2F 49
Pantheon Gdns. TN23: Kgnt 2D 38
Paper La. TN24: W'boro 1B 40
Papworth Cl. CT19: F'stone 6G 49
Parade, The CT20: F'stone 4H 5 (2C 60)
     TN24: Ashf 2B 40
Parade Rd. CT20: S'gte 4F 59
Paraker La. CT21: Hythe 3B 58
Paraker Way CT21: Hythe 4B 58
Pardoners Way CT16: Dover 6A 16
Parfitt Way CT16: Dover 1B 28
Park Av. CT14: Deal 6F 9
     CT16: Dover 1D 6 (2D 28)
Park Cl. CT18: H'nge 1G 49
Park Cnr. Cotts. TN25: Bra L 1F 43
Park Dr. TN26: Hoth 2D 30
Parker Pl. CT18: H'nge 6A 24
PARK FARM 3G 39
Park Farm Cl. CT19: F'stone 5A 50
     TN26: Shad .5C 38
Park Farm Ind. Est. CT19: F'stone 5H 49
Park Farm Retail Pk. CT19: F'stone 5H 49
Park Farm Rd. CT19: F'stone 1E 5 (5H 49)
Parkfield Rd. CT19: F'stone 2E 5 (1A 60)
Park La. CT4: Elham 1H 21
Park Mall TN24: Ashf 3B 4 (2F 35)
Park M. CT16: Dover 3D 6 (3D 28)
Park Pl. CT16: Dover 3D 6 (3D 28)
     TN23: Ashf 6F 35
     TN24: W'boro 5B 36
Park Rd. CT16: Dover 1B 28
     CT16: Temp E 4F 15
     CT19: F'stone 1E 59
     CT21: Hythe .6D 56
     TN24: Kenn .5H 31
Park Rd. Nth. TN24: Ashf 2B 4 (2F 35)
Parkside Ct. TN30: Tent 6A 64
Park St. CT14: Deal 5H 9
     CT16: Dover 3D 6 (3D 28)
     TN24: Ashf 3B 4 (3F 35)
Park Va. TN24: Kenn 5H 31
Park Vw. CT19: F'stone 6C 50
Park Vw. Ter. TN30: Tent 6A 64
Park Wood Cl. TN23: Kgnt 2F 39
Parsonage, The CT15: St Marg 3D 18
                              (off High St.)
Parsonage Farm Rd. CT15: Chu H 6E 27
Parsonage Vs. CT15: Chu H 6E 27
Parsons Way CT16: Dover 6A 16
Passage, The TN30: St Mic 2B 64
                              (off Grange Rd.)
Pasture, The CT18: H'nge 1H 49
     TN24: Kenn .5H 31
Path Fld. Cotts. CT15: W Hou 6A 26
Patterson Cl. CT14: Deal 1E 11
Paul's Pl. CT16: Dover 2C 6 (2C 28)
Pavement, The TN30: St Mic 2B 64
Pavilion Cl. CT14: Deal 3G 9
Pavilion Ct. CT20: F'stone 5H 5
Pavilion Mdw. CT17: Dover 5G 15
Pavilion M. CT19: F'stone 1F 5
Pavilion Rd. CT19: F'stone 2E 5 (1B 60)
Paxton Av. CT16: Dover 2G 49
Payers Pk. CT20: F'stone 4G 5 (2B 60)
Pay St. CT18: D'sole, H'nge 4E 23

Pearmain Way TN23: Ashf 5A 34
PEDLINGE 3H 55
PEENE 4B 48
Peene Cotts. CT18: Peene 4B 48
Peene Railway Mus. 5A 48
Pelham Gdns. CT20: F'stone 3G 59
Pemberton Ct. CT21: Hythe 4B 58
                              (off Hospital Hill)
Pemberton Rd. TN24: Ashf 3H 35
Pembroke Ct. CT20: F'stone 2H 5 (1C 60)
Pembury Ho. TN23: Ashf 1D 38
Pembury Pl. TN25: Ashf 1D 34
Pencester Ct. CT16: Dover 4F 7 (3E 29)
Pencester Rd. CT16: Dover 4E 7 (3D 28)
Penderel Ct. TN30: Tent 5B 64
                              (off Ashford Rd.)
Penderel M. TN30: Tent 5B 64
Penfold Rd. CT19: F'stone 1C 60
Penlee Point TN24: Kenn 6H 31
Penn Hill TN23: Ashf 1C 38
Pennine Way TN24: Ashf 1F 35
PENNYPOT 6B 56
Pennypot Ind. Est. CT21: Hythe 6B 56
Penrose Ct. CT21: Hythe 6E 57
Pensand Ho. CT21: Hythe 6F 57
Pent Rd. CT19: F'stone 6F 49
Pent Vale Cl. CT19: F'stone 1G 59
Percival Ter. CT17: Dover 5A 6 (4B 28)
Peregrine Cl. CT21: Hythe 1H 63
Perimeter Rd. CT16: Dover 3G 29
Perries Mead CT19: F'stone 6H 49
Perrot Way CT18: H'nge 6H 23
Perth Way CT16: Dover 6C 16
Peter Candler Way
     TN24: Kenn .1A 36
Peter St. CT14: Deal 4H 9
     CT16: Dover 3C 6 (3C 28)
     CT20: F'stone 3H 5 (2C 60)
Peto Cl. CT19: F'stone 2G 5 (1B 60)
Petrel Way CT18: H'nge 2G 49
Peverell Rd. CT16: Dover 5B 16
Pharos, The 3H 7 (3F 29)
Pharos Dr. CT16: Dover 2F 7 (2E 29)
Philippa Ho. CT19: F'stone 1D 60
Phillip Rd. CT19: F'stone 1E 59
Pier, The CT16: Whitf 1H 15
Pike Cl. CT19: F'stone 6G 49
PILGRIMS HOSPICE IN ASHFORD 6E 37
Pilgrim Spring CT19: F'stone 5A 50
Pilgrims Way CT16: Dover 6H 15
Pilots Av. CT14: Deal 1E 11
Pine Cotts. CT14: Elham 1H 21
PINEHAM 2D 16
Pineham Rd. CT15: Gus, Pine 1C 16
Pine Lodge Ct. CT14: Deal 6F 9
Pines Garden 4F 19
Pine Way CT19: F'stone 6D 48
Pioneer Rd. CT16: Dover 6A 16
Pipers Cl. CT18: Lym'ge 4E 21
Pittlesden TN30: Tent 6A 64
Pittlesden Pl. TN30: Tent 6A 64
Pittock Ho. CT14: Deal 2F 11
Pixwell La. CT14: Gt Mon 2B 10
Plain Cotts. CT20: F'stone 3G 59
Plain Rd. CT20: F'stone 3G 59
     TN25: Sme 2E 43
Plantation Cl. TN26: Hoth 1D 30
Plantin Ho. TN24: Ashf 2D 4 (2G 35)
Pleydell Ct. CT20: F'stone 6E 5
Pleydell Gdns. CT20: F'stone 6F 5 (3B 60)
Plimsoll Av. CT19: F'stone 5B 50
Plough Hill CT15: Chu H 1E 53
Ploughmans Way TN23: Kgnt 2B 38
Plover Rd. CT18: H'nge 2F 49
Plumpton Rd. TN25: Hin 4H 37
Pluto Ho. TN23: Ashf 4D 4 (3G 35)
Poets Wlk. CT14: Walm 4F 11
Pollard Cl. TN23: Ashf 5D 34
Pommeus La. CT14: Ripp 6B 10
Poncia Rd. TN23: Ashf 6E 35
Pond Hill Rd. CT20: F'stone 2C 58
Pond La. CT15: St Marg 2B 18
Pondmore Way TN25: Ashf 1D 34
Pope Ho. La. TN30: St Mic 1B 64
Poplar CT. TN23: Ashf 2D 34
Poplars, The TN23: Ashf 6E 35
Poppy Mead TN23: Kgnt 5G 39
Portland Cl. CT21: Hythe 5D 56
     TN24: Kenn 4F 31

Portland Ct. CT21: Hythe 5D **56**
(off Portland Cl.)
Portland Rd. CT21: Hythe 5D **56**
(not continuous)
Port Lympne Wild Animal Pk. 5B **54**
Portobello Ct. CT14: Deal 4H **9**
POSTLING 2B **46**
Postling TN23: Ashf 4C **34**
Postling Ct. CT21: Post 3A **46**
Postling Rd. CT19: F'stone 6E **49**
Potters Cl. TN25: Ashf 5C **30**
POTTERS CORNER 5C **30**
Poulton Cl. CT17: Dover 2G **27**
Poulton Cl. Bus. Pk. CT17: Dover 2G **27**
Pound Ct. TN23: Kgnt 4E **39**
Poundfield Wlk. TN23: Ashf 5B **34**
(not continuous)
Pound Ho. TN23: Ashf 5F **35**
Pound La. CT4: Elham 2H **21**
TN23: Kgnt .2D **38**
TN25: Bra L, Sme 1F **43**
Pound Way CT19: F'stone 5G **5** (3B **60**)
Prescott Cl. CT15: Gus 3E **17**
Primrose Dr. TN23: Kgnt 3F **39**
Primrose Pl. CT17: Dover 2B **28**
Primrose Rd. CT17: Dover 2A **28**
Prince of Wales Ho. CT17: Dover 5D **6**
Prince of Wales Res. Pk. CT21: Hythe . . .6A **56**
Prince of Wales Rdbt. CT17: Dover 5D **28**
Prince of Wales Ter. CT14: Deal 6H **9**
Princes Ga. CT20: F'stone 5G **5**
Princes Pde. CT17: Dover 6F **57**
Princess of Wales's Royal Regiment Mus.
. . . . .3E **29**
(within Dover Castle)
Princess St. CT19: F'stone 1H **5** (1C **60**)
Princes St. CT14: Deal 4H **9**
CT17: Dover 5E **7** (4D **28**)
Princes Ter. CT21: Hythe 6B **56**
Prince William Ct. CT14: Deal 4H **9**
Prioress Wlk. CT16: Dover 6A **16**
Priors Lees CT20: F'stone 6F **5** (3B **60**)
Priory Gdns. CT20: F'stone 5G **5** (3B **60**)
Priory Ga. Rd. CT17: Dover 4C **6** (3C **28**)
Priory Gro. CT17: Dover 4C **6** (3C **28**)
Priory Hill CT17: Dover 4B **6** (3C **28**)
Priory Ho. CT17: Dover 6B **6** (4C **28**)
Priory La. TN25: M Hor 1A **44**
Priory Pl. CT17: Dover 3C **28**
Priory Rd. CT17: Dover 4D **6** (3D **28**)
Priory Station App. Rd.
CT17: Dover 5C **6** (3C **28**)
Priory St. CT17: Tent 4D **6** (3D **28**)
Priory Way TN30: Tent 6C **64**
Pritchard Dr. CT18: H'nge 1G **49**
Probyn M. CT18: H'nge 2F **49**
Proctor Wlk. CT18: H'nge 1F **49**
Promenade CT14: Deal 2H **9**
CT14: Walm 1H **11**
CT16: Dover 6F **7** (4E **29**)
Prospect M. CT21: Hythe 5E **57**
Prospect Pl. CT17: Dover 2A **6** (2B **28**)
Prospect Rd. CT20: S'gte 4D **58**
CT21: Hythe 5E **57**
Prospect Ter. CT4: Elham 1H **21**
Prospect Way TN25: Bra L 1E **43**
Providence St. TN23: Ashf 5G **35**
Puffin Ct. CT18: H'nge 2G **49**

Q

Quain Ct. CT20: F'stone 3A **60**
Quantock Dr. TN24: Ashf . . . .2A **4** & 1B **4** (2F **35**)
Quarrington La. TN25: W Bra . . .5G **37** & 6H **37**
Quarry Cl. TN24: W'boro 5B **36**
Quarry La. CT21: Hythe 4D **56**
Quarry Rd. CT21: Hythe 4D **56**
Quarry Vw. TN23: Ashf 6B **34**
Quarry Wlk. CT21: Hythe 4A **58**
Quebec Ter. CT16: Dover 6B **16**
(off Winnipeg Cl.)
Queen Elizabeth Rd. CT16: Dover . . .4H **7** (3F **29**)
Queen Mother Ct. CT14: Walm 4H **11**
Queens Av. CT17: Dover 2B **28**
CT20: F'stone 1B **58**
Queens Ct. CT21: Hythe 6D **56**
(off Albert Rd.)
TN24: Ashf 2C **4** (2G **35**)

Queens Courtyard CT17: Dover 4E **7**
Queensdown Rd. CT14: Kgdn 3G **13**
Queens Gdns. CT17: Dover 4E **7** (3D **28**)
Queen's Lea CT15: W Hou 6A **26**
Queens M. CT14: Deal 5H **9**
Queen's Ri. CT14: R'wld 2D **12**
Queens Rd. TN24: W'boro 4C **36**
Queen St. CT14: Deal 5G **9**
CT17: Dover 5E **7** (4D **28**)
CT20: F'stone 3H **5** (2C **60**)
TN23: Ashf 4B **4** (3F **35**)
Queen St. M. TN23: Ashf 4B **4**
Queen Victoria Row CT16: Dover 3D **6**
Quern Rd. CT14: Deal 2E **11**
Quested Rd. CT19: F'stone 1E **59**

R

Radcliffe Ct. CT21: Hythe 5D **56**
Radnor Bri. Rd. CT19: F'stone 3H **5** (2C **60**)
CT20: F'stone 3H **5** (2C **60**)
Radnor Chambers CT20: F'stone 5F **5**
Radnor Cliff CT20: F'stone 4G **59**
Radnor Cliff Cres. CT20: F'stone 4G **59**
Radnor Pk. Av. CT19: F'stone 2E **5** (1H **59**)
Radnor Pk. Cres. CT19: F'stone . . .3E **5** (2A **60**)
Radnor Pk. Gdns. CT19: F'stone . . .2E **5** (1A **60**)
Radnor Pk. Rd. CT19: F'stone 2E **5** (2A **60**)
Radnor Pk. W. CT19: F'stone 2H **59**
Radnor St. CT19: F'stone 4H **5** (2C **60**)
Raleigh Cl. TN24: W'boro 5C **36**
Ramp A CT16: Dover 3H **29**
Rampart Rd. CT21: Hythe 5D **56**
Ramp B CT16: Dover 3H **29**
Ramp C CT16: Dover 3G **29**
Ramstone Cl. TN25: Sme 2E **43**
Randolph Gdns. TN24: Kenn 6A **32**
Randolph Ho. CT20: F'stone 4H **5**
(off The Tram Rd.)
Randolph Rd. CT17: Dover 2A **28**
Ranelagh Rd. CT14: Deal 6H **9**
Range Rd. CT21: Hythe 6D **56**
Range Rd. Ind. Est. CT21: Hythe 6C **56**
Ravenlea Rd. CT20: F'stone 2G **59**
Ravenscourt Rd. CT14: Deal 6G **9**
Raymond Ct. Cotts. TN25: Brook 5F **33**
Raymond Fuller Way TN24: Kenn 1A **36**
Rayworth Ct. TN24: W'boro 5A **36**
Reach Cl. CT15: St Marg 3D **18**
Reachfields CT21: Hythe 6C **56**
Reach Mdw. CT15: St Marg 3E **19**
Reach Rd. CT15: St Marg 4D **18**
CT21: Lymp 4E **55**
Readers Bri. Rd. TN30: St Mic 2A **64**
Reading Cl. CT14: Walm 4F **11**
Reading Rd. CT17: Dover 4H **27**
Recreation Ground Rd. TN30: Tent 6B **64**
Rectory Bungs. TN26: Shad 6C **38**
Rectory La. CT18: Lym'ge 5E **21**
CT21: Salt .3D **56**
Rectory Rd. CT14: Deal 1D **10**
Rectory Way TN24: Kenn 6G **31**
Redbarn La. CT15: Ewe M 6A **14**
Redberry Rd. TN23: Kgnt 2F **39**
Redbrooks Way CT21: Hythe 4B **56**
Redhouse Wall CT14: Deal 2F **9**
Redington TN24: Ashf 2C **4** (2G **35**)
Redlands Ct. CT17: Dover 5G **15**
Red Lion Sq. CT21: Hythe 5D **56**
Redmill Cl. CT20: F'stone 2E **59**
Redoubt Sailing Club 1G **63**
Redoubt Way TN29: Dym 4F **63**
Redsull Av. CT14: Deal 2E **11**
Red Tree Orchard TN23: Ashf 6C **34**
Redvers Cotts. CT16: Dover 4G **15**
Redwing Cl. CT18: H'nge 2G **49**
Redyear Ct. TN24: W'boro 4H **36**
Reece Adams Ho. CT18: Cap F 4E **51**
Reed Cres. TN23: Kgnt 4G **39**
Reedmace Cl. TN23: Ashf 5B **34**
Regents Ct. TN23: Ashf 3A **4**
Regents Pl. TN23: Ashf 3A **4** (3F **35**)
Remus Cl. TN23: Kgnt 3D **38**
Remus Ho. CT17: Dover 3C **28**
Rendezvous St. CT20: F'stone 4G **5** (3B **60**)
(not continuous)
Repton Av. TN23: Ashf 1D **34**
Repton Mnr. Rd. TN23: Ashf 2E **35**

Residences, The CT17: Dover 4E **7**
(off Worthington St.)
RHODES MINNIS 1C **20**
Ribston Way TN23: Ashf 6A **34**
Richard Hillary Cl. TN24: W'boro 1H **39**
Richborough Way CT21: Kgnt 2C **38**
Richmond Ct. CT14: Walm 1H **11**
CT16: Dover 2E **7** (2D **28**)
(off Trafalgar Dr.)
Richmond Ho. CT20: F'stone 4H **5**
Richmond Meech Dr. TN24: Kenn 1A **36**
Richmond St. CT19: F'stone 1D **58**
Ridge, The TN24: Kenn 5A **32**
RIDGE ROW .2F **23**
Ridgeway, The CT17: Dover 1G **27**
CT21: Lymp 4E **55**
TN25: Sme .3A **42**
Ridgeway Ter. TN25: Sme 2C **42**
Riding Hill TN24: Kenn 5G **31**
Ridley Cl. CT18: H'nge 2F **49**
Rigden Rd. TN23: Ashf 6F **35**
RINGWOULD .2D **12**
Ringwould Rd. CT14: Kgdn, R'wld 2E **13**
CT14: Mart, Ripp 4A **12**
CT15: Mart .4A **12**
Ripley Rd. TN24: W'boro 5C **36**
RIPPLE 5B **10**
Ripple Rd. CT14: Ripp, Walm 1C **12**
Risborough La. CT19: F'stone 2D **58**
CT20: F'stone 2D **58**
Risborough Way CT20: F'stone 1E **59**
Rise, The CT14: Kgdn 2G **13**
CT15: St Marg 3F **19**
TN23: Ashf .6C **34**
Rising Rd. TN23: Ashf 4E **35**
RIVER 6G **15**
Riverbank Way TN24: W'boro 1H **39**
River Ct. CT17: Dover 1H **27**
Riverdale CT17: Dover 6H **15**
River Dr. CT17: Dover 1H **27**
River Mdw. CT17: Dover 6H **15**
Riversdale Rd. TN23: Ashf 5G **35**
Riverside CT16: Temp E 4E **15**
CT17: Dover 6H **15**
Riverside Bus. Pk. TN24: Ashf 3H **35**
Riverside Cl. TN23: Kgnt 3E **39**
Riverside Ind. Est. CT21: W Hyt 6F **55**
Riverside Trad. Est. TN23: Ashf 4D **35**
River St. CT17: Dover 6G **15**
Riverview TN23: Ashf 4C **34**
Riviera, The CT20: S'gte 4F **59**
Riviera Ct. CT20: S'gte 4E **59**
Road of Remembrance
CT20: F'stone 5G **5** (3B **60**)
Robert Brundett Cl. TN24: Kenn 6A **32**
Robert St. CT14: Deal 4H **9**
Robin's Cl. CT21: Hythe 1G **63**
Robson's Yd. CT17: Dover 3B **6**
Robus Cl. CT18: Lym'ge 4E **21**
Robus Ter. CT18: Lym'ge 4E **21**
Roderick Kalberer Pl.
TN23: Ashf .2C **34**
Roethorne Gdns. TN30: Tent 5B **64**
Rogersmead TN30: Tent 6A **64**
Rokesley Rd. CT16: Dover 4B **16**
Rolvenden Rd. TN30: Tent 6A **64**
Roman Cl. CT14: Deal 5F **9**
Roman Painted House, The 5E **7**
Roman Rd. CT15: Pine 1D **16**
CT16: Dover 1D **28**
Roman Way CT15: St Marg 4D **18**
CT19: F'stone 1C **58**
TN23: Kgnt .3F **39**
Romney Av. CT20: F'stone 2F **59**
Romney, Hythe & Dymchurch Railway
Hythe Station 5C **56**
Romney Marsh Rd.
TN23: Ashf, Kgnt 6C **4** (4G **35**)
Romney Point TN23: Ashf 1D **34**
Romney Rd. TN24: W'boro 4A **36**
Romney Way CT21: Hythe 6B **56**
Romsey Cl. TN24: W'boro 3C **36**
Romulus Gdns. TN23: Kgnt 3D **38**
Rookery Cl. TN23: Kenn 4H **31**
Roosevelt Rd. CT16: Dover 6B **16**
Rosamund Ct. CT19: F'stone 1E **5**
Rose Ct. CT17: Dover 2B **28**
(off Primrose Rd.)
Roselands CT14: Walm 4G **11**

Rosemary Vs. CT20: F'stone 2C **60**
(off Saffron's Pl.)
Rose Wlk. CT18: H'nge 1G **49**
Rosewood Dr. TN25: Ashf 1C **34**
Ross Ct. TN23: Ashf 1E **39**
Rossendale Ct. CT20: F'stone 2H **5**
Rossendale Gdns. CT20: F'stone . . .2H **5** (1C **60**)
Rossendale Rd. CT20: F'stone . . .2H **5** (1C **60**)
Ross Way CT20: F'stone 2E **59**
Rothbrook Dr. TN24: Kenn 4G **31**
Rothbury Gdns. CT21: Hythe 5B **56**
Rothley Cl. TN30: Tent 5B **64**
Roundhill Tunnel CT19: F'stone 4H **49**
Row, The CT4: Elham 2H **21**
Rowan Cl. TN23: Ashf 3C **34**
Rowland Cotts. CT21: Lymp 4D **54**
Royal Cinque Ports Golf Course 2G **9**
Royal Cinque Ports Yacht Club 6F **7**
Royal Military Av. CT20: F'stone 3D **58**
Royal Military Rd. CT21: Hythe, W Hyt . . .6A **54**
ROYAL VICTORIA HOSPITAL 2E **5** (1A **60**)
Royal Victoria Pl. CT16: Dover 3D **6**
Royds Rd. TN24: W'boro 1H **39**
Royston Gdns. CT15: St Marg 3D **18**
Ruffetts Wood TN23: Kgnt 4G **39**
Rugby Gdns. TN23: Ashf 5G **35**
Rugby Rd. CT17: Dover 5A **28**
Running Foxes La. TN23: Ashf 6B **34**
Rural Ter. TN25: Wye 1G **33**
Russell Rd. CT19: F'stone . . .1F **5** (1B **60**)
Russell St. CT16: Dover 4F **7** (3E **29**)
Russett Cl. TN23: Ashf 6A **34**
Rutherford Rd. TN25: Ashf 6F **31**
Rutland Rd. CT16: Dover 6B **16**
Rutledge Av. TN25: Mers 5H **39**
Rye Ct. TN23: Ashf 6B **34**
Ryland Ct. CT20: F'stone 3H **5**
Ryland Pl. CT20: F'stone 3H **5** (2C **60**)
Rylands Rd. TN24: Kenn 5H **31**

S

Sabre Cres. TN23: Ashf 6B **34**
Sackville Cl. TN26: Hoth 1D **30**
Sackville Cres. TN23: Ashf 3E **35**
Saddlers, The TN25: S'ndge 6H **43**
Saddlers Way TN23: Kgnt 2F **39**
Saffron's Pl. CT20: F'stone 4H **5** (2C **60**)
St Alphege Rd. CT16: Dover 1C **6** (2C **28**)
St Ambrose Grn. TN25: Wye 1G **33**
St Andrews CT19: F'stone 2C **60**
St Andrew's Cl. CT19: F'stone 6H **49**
St Andrews Gdns. CT17: Dover 1A **28**
St Andrew's Rd. CT14: Deal 5G **9**
St Andrew Ter. CT17: Dover 1A **28**
St Anne's Rd. TN23: Ashf 6D **34**
St Augustine's Rd. CT14: Deal 1D **10**
St Barnabas Cl. TN23: Ashf 6D **34**
St Bartholomew's Cl.
CT17: Dover 3B **6** (3C **28**)
St Bartholomews Ct. CT17: Dover 4A **6**
(off Curzon Rd.)
St Benets Ct. TN30: Tent 5B **64**
St Benets Way TN30: Tent 5B **64**
St Clare Rd. CT14: Walm 4G **11**
St Clements Ct. CT19: F'stone 2D **60**
St David's Av. CT17: Dover . . .1H **53** & 6A **28**
St David's Rd. CT14: Deal 5G **9**
St Denys Rd. CT18: H'nge 6H **23**
St Eanswythe's M. CT20: F'stone 4H **5**
St Eanswythe Way CT20: F'stone . .4G **5** (2B **60**)
St Edmund's Rd. CT14: Deal 1C **10**
St Edmunds Wlk. CT17: Dover 4D **6**
(off Biggin St.)
St Francis Cl. CT14: Deal 1C **10**
St Francis Ct. TN23: Ashf 6D **34**
St Francis Rd. CT19: F'stone 1F **59**
St Gabriel's Cl. CT20: F'stone 3H **5**
St Georges Bus. Cen. TN23: Ashf 3D **34**
St Georges Cl. CT17: Dover 1A **28**
St George's Cres. CT17: Dover 6B **28**
St George's Pas. CT14: Deal 5H **9**
St Georges Pl. CT15: St Marg 3D **18**
CT21: Hythe 1H **63**
St Georges Rd. CT14: Deal 5G **9**
CT19: F'stone 1F **59**
St Georges Sq. TN23: Ashf 3B **4**
St Georges Ter. CT19: F'stone 1F **59**

St Giles Cl. CT17: Dover 6B **28**
St Giles Rd. CT17: Dover 6B **28**
St Giles Wlk. CT17: Dover 6B **28**
St Gregory's Cl. CT14: Deal 1D **10**
St Hilda Rd. CT19: F'stone 1E **59**
St Hildas Rd. CT21: Hythe 6D **56**
St Hugh Ter. CT18: H'nge 1F **49**
(off St Michael's Wlk.)
St James Cl. CT14: Deal 2F **11**
St James La. CT16: Dover 5F **7** (4E **29**)
St James Rd. CT14: Kgdn 2H **13**
St James's Church 4G **7** (3E **29**)
St James St. CT16: Dover 5F **7** (4E **29**)
(not continuous)
St John's Chu. Rd. CT19: F'stone . . .2E **5** (1A **60**)
St John's Cl. CT18: D'sole 4G **23**
St John's Ct. TN24: Svgtn 6C **36**
St Johns La. TN23: Ashf 4C **4** (3G **35**)
St John's Rd. CT17: Dover 5C **6** (4C **28**)
CT21: Hythe 6D **56**
St John's St. CT20: F'stone 3G **5** (2B **60**)
St John's Ter. CT19: F'stone 2F **5**
St John's Way CT18: D'sole 4F **23**
St Lawrence Ter. CT16: Dover 6B **16**
(off Montreal Cl.)
St Leonard's Church Crypt 5E **57**
St Leonard's Rd. CT21: Hythe 6D **56**
(off St Leonard's Rd.)
St Leonard's M. CT21: Hythe 6D **56**
St Leonard's Rd. CT14: Deal 1F **11**
CT21: Hythe 6D **56**
St Luke's Wlk. CT18: H'nge 1F **49**
ST MARGARET'S AT CLIFFE 3D **18**
St Margarets Bay CT15: St Marg 3C **18**
St Margarets Ct. CT20: F'stone 2H **59**
St Margarets Dr. CT14: Walm 4F **11**
St Margaret's Mus. 4F **19**
St Margarets Rd. CT15: St Marg 5E **13**
(Collingwood Rd. E.)
CT15: St Marg 4E **19**
(Foreland Rd.)
St Marks Cl. CT20: F'stone 2D **58**
St Martin's Cl. CT17: Dover 6B **28**
St Martins Gdns. CT17: Dover 5C **6**
St Martin's Path CT17: Dover 5C **28**
ST MARTIN'S PLAIN 1B **58**
St Martins Rd. CT14: Deal 1D **10**
CT15: Gus 5E **17**
CT20: F'stone 1D **58**
St Martin's Steps CT17: Dover 5C **28**
St Mary in Castro Church 3H **7** (3F **29**)
St Mary's Cl. CT18: Etch'l 2F **47**
St Mary's Dr. CT18: Etch'l 2F **47**
St Mary's Grn. TN24: Kenn 4A **32**
St Mary's M. TN24: W'boro 5B **36**
St Mary's Pas. CT16: Dover 5E **7** (3D **28**)
St Mary's Rd. CT4: Elham 2H **21**
CT14: Walm 4G **11**
CT21: W Hyt 6F **55**
St Mary's Ter. CT20: F'stone 2H **5**
ST MICHAELS 2B **64**
St Michael's Ct. CT20: F'stone 3H **5**
St Michaels St. CT20: F'stone . . .3G **5** (2C **60**)
St Michael's Ter. TN30: St Mic 2A **64**
St Michael's Wlk. CT18: H'nge 1F **49**
(not continuous)
St Mildreds Rd. TN30: Tent 6A **64**
St Mildreds Ct. CT14: Walm 4G **11**
St Monicas CT17: Dover 5B **6** (4C **28**)
St Monica's Rd. CT14: Kgdn 1H **13**
St Nicholas Cl. CT14: Deal 1D **10**
St Nicholas Rd. CT21: Hythe 5C **56**
St Nicholas Ter. CT21: Hythe 5D **56**
St Patrick's Cl. CT14: Deal 5G **9**
St Patrick's Rd. CT14: Deal 5G **9**
CT17: Dover 6A **28**
St Paul's Ct. CT20: S'gte 3E **59**
St Paul's Way CT20: F'stone 3E **59**
St Peter's Way TN26: Shad 6C **38**
ST RADIGUND'S 1A **6** (2A **28**)
St Radigund's Abbey Farm Cotts.
CT15: Guston 2C **26**
(not continuous)
St Radigund's Ct. CT17: Dover 2A **28**
St Radigund's Rd. CT17: Dover . . .1A **6** (2H **27**)
St Radigunds Wlk. CT17: Dover 1A **6**
(off Bunkers Hill Av.)
St Richard's Rd. CT14: Deal 1C **10**
St Richard's Wlk. CT17: Dover 1H **53**

St Saviours Cl. CT19: F'stone 6B **50**
ST SAVIOUR'S SPIRE HOSPITAL 5H **57**
St Stephens M. TN23: Ashf 1E **39**
St Stephen's Wlk. TN23: Ashf 6D **34**
St Stephen's Way CT20: F'stone 3F **59**
St Teresa's Cl.
TN24: Ashf 2A **4** (2F **35**)
St Vincent Rd. CT15: St Marg 2C **18**
St Winifred Rd. CT19: F'stone 1F **59**
Salisbury Rd. CT14: Walm 3F **11**
CT15: St Marg 3F **19**
CT16: Dover 2C **6** (2C **28**)
CT19: F'stone 6E **49**
SALTWOOD .3D **56**
Samian Cres. CT19: F'stone 1C **58**
Samphire Ct. CT16: Dover 3F **7** (3E **29**)
Samphire Hoe 3F **53**
Samphire Rd. CT17: Dover 2G **53**
Sanctuary Cl. CT17: Dover 5F **15**
SANDGATE .4E **59**
Sandgate Castle 4F **59**
Sandgate High St.
CT20: S'gte 4E **59**
Sandgate Hill CT20: S'gte 4F **59**
Sandgate Rd. CT20: F'stone 6E **5** (3G **59**)
Sandhill Caravan Pk. CT14: Deal 2F **9**
Sandilands TN24: W'boro 4A **36**
Sandling Rd. CT18: Lym'ge 2C **46**
CT21: Post 5B **46**
CT21: Salt, S'Ing 6A **46**
Sandlings, The CT21: Salt 3D **56**
Sandling Station (Rail) 1B **56**
Sandown Cl. CT14: Deal 2H **9**
Sandown Pl. CT14: Deal 4H **9**
Sandown Rd. CT14: Deal 2H **9**
Sandpiper Ct. CT16: Dover 1B **28**
Sandpiper Rd. CT18: H'nge 2G **49**
Sandstone Ct. CT20: F'stone 4G **59**
Sandwich Cl. CT20: F'stone 2F **59**
Sandwich Rd. CT14: Hackl, Shol 1A **8**
(not continuous)
CT16: Whitf 3A **16**
Sandyhurst La. TN25: Ashf, Hoth 5C **30**
TN26: Ashf 5C **30**
Sandy La. CT21: Hythe 4B **58**
TN24: W'boro 3D **36**
TN30: Tent 6B **64**
Sandy Pl. TN25: Sme 2D **42**
Sassoon Cl. CT18: H'nge 1F **49**
SATMAR 2H **51**
Satmar Cl. CT15: Cap F, W Hou 2H **51**
CT18: Cap F, W Hou 2H **51**
Satmore La. CT18: Cap F 1G **51**
Saturn Ho. TN23: Ashf 5C **4** (4G **35**)
Saw Lodge Fld. TN23: Kgnt 3G **39**
Saxon Cl. CT21: Hythe 5G **57**
Saxon Ho. CT20: F'stone 3H **5**
Saxons Cl. CT14: Deal 3G **9**
Saxon St. CT17: Dover 4D **6** (3D **28**)
Sayers La. TN30: Tent 6A **64**
Scanlons Bri. Rd. CT21: Hythe 5C **56**
School La. CT18: N'tn 6A **48**
School Rd. CT18: Acr 4E **23**
CT21: Hythe, Salt 3D **56**
TN26: Hoth 1D **30**
Scotland Comn. CT16: Temp E 4E **15**
Scotney La. TN25: Mers 5H **39**
Scotton St. TN25: Wye 1H **33**
SEABROOK 5B **58**
Seabrook Ct. CT21: Hythe 4B **58**
Seabrook Gdns. CT21: Hythe 5A **58**
Seabrook Mt. CT21: Hythe 4A **58**
Seabrook Rd. CT21: Hythe 5F **57**
Seabrook Va. CT21: Hythe 3B **58**
Seadown Cl. CT21: Hythe 3A **58**
Sea Rd. CT14: Kgdn 1G **13**
CT21: Hythe 5G **57**
(Cannongate Cl.)
CT21: Hythe 5H **57**
(Ferguson Cl.)
CT21: Hythe 5A **58**
(Seabrook Gro.)
Seascape CT20: S'gte 4E **59**
(off Gough Rd.)
Sea St. CT15: St Marg 3E **19**
Seaton Av. CT21: Hythe 4D **56**
Sea Vw. Cl. CT18: Cap F 4F **51**
Sea Vw. Rd. CT15: St Marg 5D **18**

Sea Vw. Ter. CT17: Dover 1A 28
CT20: S'gte 4D 58
(off Wellington Pl.)
Sea Wlk. CT20: S'gte 4E 59
Secret Wartime Tunnels 3H 7 (2F 29)
Segrave Cres. CT19: F'stone 1D 60
Segrave Rd. CT19: F'stone 2D 60
Selborne Ho. CT17: Dover 6A 6
Selbourne Ter. CT17: Dover 6C 6 (4C 28)
Selby Field Caravan Pk. CT21: W Hyt . . .1B 62
Selkirk Rd. CT16: Dover 6B 16
SELLINDGE 5B 44
Selway Ct. CT14: Deal 2F 11
Sene Pk. CT21: Hythe 4F 57
Sene Valley Golf Course 3G 57
Setterfield Ho. CT21: Hythe 5F 57
SEVINGTON 1D 40
Sevington La. TN24: W'boro 5B 36
Seymour Rd. CT15: St Marg 1D 18
SHADOXHURST 6C 38
Shaftesbury Av. CT19: F'stone 6D 48
Shaftesbury Ct. CT14: Walm 3H 11
Shakespeare Rd. CT17: Dover 5B 28
Shakespeare Ter. CT20: F'stone 6E 5 (3A 60)
Shaw Cross TN24: Kenn 6H 31
Shear Way TN29: Burm 4A 62
Shearway Bus. Pk. CT19: F'stone 6F 49
(not continuous)
Shearway Rd. CT19: F'stone 5F 49
Sheepfold La. TN23: Kgnt 4G 39
Sheffield Gdns. CT14: Walm 1G 11
Sheldwich Cl. TN23: Ashf 1D 38
Shellons St. CT20: F'stone 4F 5 (2B 60)
Shephard Ho. CT20: F'stone 4F 5
Shepherd Cl. TN23: Kgnt 2C 38
Shepherd Dr. TN24: W'boro 5C 36
Shepherds Wlk. CT21: Hythe 6A 56
Shepway TN24: Kenn 6A 32
Shepway Cl. CT19: F'stone 2F 5 (1B 60)
Sheridan Rd. CT16: Dover 6B 16
Sheron Cl. CT14: Deal 6E 9
Sherwood Dr. TN24: Kenn 4H 31
Sherwood Trust Homes CT20: F'stone 3H 5
(off St Michaels La.)
Shipley Mill Cl. TN23: Kgnt 3G 39
Shipman's Way CT16: Dover 6A 16
Ship St. CT19: F'stone 3F 5 (2B 60)
Shireway Cl. CT19: F'stone 6G 49
SHOLDEN 5D 8
Sholden Bank CT14: Gt Mon 1C 10
Sholden New Rd. CT14: Shol 5D 8
Shooter's Hill CT17: Dover 2B 6 (2C 28)
Shoreham La. TN30: St Mic 2A 64
Shorncliffe Cres. CT20: F'stone 2E 59
Shorncliffe Ind. Est. CT20: F'stone 2E 59
Shorncliffe Rd. CT20: F'stone 4E 5 (2E 59)
Short La. CT15: Alk 2H 25
Shrubbery, The CT14: Walm 4G 11
Shrubcote TN30: Tent 6C 64
(not continuous)
SHUTTLESFIELD 4A 22
Shuttlesfield La. CT4: O'nge 2F 21
Sidings, The CT18: Lym'ge 4E 21
Sidney St. CT19: F'stone 1H 5 (1C 60)
Silecroft Ct. TN23: Ashf 4C 34
Silver Birch Gro. TN23: Kgnt 3F 39
Silver Hill TN30: St Mic, Tent 4B 64
Silver Hill Gdns. CT14: Walm 4C 36
Silver Hill Rd. TN24: W'boro 4C 36
Silverlands Rd. CT18: Lym'ge 4D 20
Silver Screen Cinema
Dover 5E 7 (4D 28)
Folkestone 4G 5 (2B 60)
Silver St. CT14: Deal 4H 9
Simone Weil Av. TN24: Ashf 1E 35
Simon's Av. TN23: Ashf 6D 34
Sincoe Ter. CT16: Dover 6B 16
(off Toronto Cl.)
Singledge Av. CT16: Whitf 3H 15
Singledge La. CT15: Cold, Whitf 1F 15
CT16: Whitf 1F 15
SINGLETON 5B 34
Singleton Centre, The TN23: Ashf 5B 34
Singleton Hill TN23: Ashf 6A 34
Singleton Rd. CT14: Gt Cha 4A 34
Sir Bernard Paget Av. TN23: Ashf 2D 34
Sir Henry Brackenbury Rd. TN23: Ashf . . .2C 34
Sir John Fogge Av. TN23: Ashf 1D 34
Sir John Moore Av. CT21: Hythe 5C 56

Sir John Moore Ct. CT20: S'gte 4E 59
Siskin Cl. CT18: H'nge 1F 49
TN25: Kenn 4F 31
Six Flds. Path TN30: Tent 6A 64
SKEETE 4A 20
Skeete Rd. CT18: Lym'ge 4A 20
Skylark Way TN23: Kgnt 4H 39
Slip La. CT15: Alk 1F 25
Slip Pas. CT17: Dover 6F 7 (4D 28)
Smallhythe Rd. TN30: Tent 6A 64
SMEETH 3C 42
Smithy Dr. TN23: Kgnt 1H 39
Snargate St. CT17: Dover 6D 6 (5D 28)
Snelgrove Ho. CT16: Dover 3E 7 (3D 28)
Snipe Cl. TN25: Kenn 4G 31
Snowbell Rd. TN23: Kgnt 3F 39
Snowdrop Cl. CT19: F'stone 5A 50
Soloman Ho. CT14: Deal 2F 11
Solton La. CT15: E Lan 1G 17
Somerfield Barn Ct. TN25: S'ndge 5A 44
Somerset Ct. CT14: Walm 2F 11
Somerset Rd. CT14: Walm 2G 11
CT19: F'stone 1E 59
TN24: Ashf 3B 4 (3F 35)
Sondes Rd. CT14: Deal 6H 9
Sotherton TN24: W'boro 6A 36
Souberg Cl. CT14: Deal 3G 11
SOUTH ALKHAM 3F 25
SOUTH ASHFORD 5F 35
Southbourne TN23: Ashf 2C 38
Southbourne Rd. CT19: F'stone 2C 60
Sth. Camber Way CT16: Dover 3H 29
South Ct. CT14: Deal 5H 9
Southdown Cl. TN25: Kenn 5A 40
Southenay La. TN25: S'ndge 4G 43
Southern Way CT20: F'stone 2H 5 (1C 60)
Southernwood Ri. CT20: F'stone 3F 59
Sth. Exit Rd. CT16: Dover 3G 29
South Foreland Lighthouse 6D 18
South Foreland Valley 5E 19
Southgate Rd. TN30: Tent 6C 64
Sth. Goodwin Ct. CT14: Deal 3H 9
South Lea TN23: Kgnt 6E 39
Southmead Cl. CT19: F'stone 1G 59
Sth. Military Rd. CT17: Dover 6C 28
South Motto TN23: Kgnt 3F 39
South Prom. CT14: Deal 5H 9
South Rd. CT14: Kgdn 2H 13
CT17: Dover 3A 6 (3B 28)
CT20: F'stone 4C 58
CT21: Hythe 6E 57
Southstone Ct. CT21: Hythe 6E 57
SOUTH STOUR .6C 40
Sth. Stour Av. TN23: Ashf 5G 35
South St. CT14: Deal 5H 9
CT20: F'stone 4H 5 (2C 60)
South Wall CT14: Deal 3E 9
Southwall Ind. Est. CT14: Deal 4F 9
Southwall Rd. CT14: Deal 4F 9
SOUTH WILLESBOROUGH 6A 36
SOVAL 5E 27
Spade Ho. CT20: S'gte 4F 59
(off Radnor Cliff Cres.)
Spanton Cres. CT21: Hythe 4C 56
Spartan Rd. TN23: Ashf 5A 34
Spelders Hill TN25: Brook 2H 37
Speldhurst Cl. TN23: Ashf 2C 38
Spence Cl. CT18: H'nge 1G 49
Spencer Cl. CT20: S'gte 4C 58
Spencer Ho. CT20: F'stone 2F 59
(off Coolinge La.)
Spicers Ct. CT21: Hythe 6E 57
Spindlewood End TN23: Ashf 1B 34
Spinney, The CT17: Dover 1G 27
TN23: Ashf 2C 34
Spitfire Way CT18: H'nge 6G 23
Split Ho. CT17: Dover 2A 28
Springfield Av. TN30: St Mic 3C 64
Springfield Pas. CT21: Hythe 5D 56
Springfield Rd. CT16: Dover 1B 28
Springfield Way CT21: Hythe 4B 58
Spring Ho. Flats CT21: Hythe 5E 57
(off Dental St.)
Spring La. CT21: Hythe 3A 58
Springside La. CT18: Lym'ge 5E 21
Spring Ter. CT20: F'stone 4G 5
(off Dover Rd.)
Springwood Cl. TN23: Ashf 2C 34
Springwood Dr. TN23: Ashf 2B 34

Sprotlands Av. TN24: W'boro 4B 36
Square, The CT4: Elham 2H 21
Squires Way CT16: Dover 6A 16
Squirrel La. TN25: Ashf 6D 30
Stable Ct. CT17: Dover 3B 6
Stable Mead CT19: F'stone 6G 49
Stable M. CT18: Etch'l 1F 47
Stace Cl. TN30: Tent 5C 64
Stade, The CT19: F'stone 4H 5 (2C 60)
Stade St. CT21: Hythe 6E 57
Stafford Cl. TN23: Ashf 3D 34
Stag Ent. Pk. TN33: Ashf 4E 35
Stanbury Cres. CT19: F'stone 6D 50
Standen La. CT18: H'nge 6B 24
STANFORD 4F 45
STANHOPE 1D 38
Stanhope Ct. TN23: Ashf 1D 38
Stanhope Rd. CT14: Deal 5H 9
CT16: Dover 1C 6 (1C 28)
TN23: Ashf 1C 38
Stanhope Sq. TN23: Ashf 1D 38
Stanhope Vs. TN23: Kgnt 2E 39
Stanley Cl. TN29: Dym 5F 63
Stanley Ct. CT14: Deal 6H 9
CT19: F'stone 1E 59
Stansfeld Av. CT18: H'nge 1G 49
Staple La. CT21: Post 2B 46
Star La. CT19: F'stone 6D 48
Star Rd. TN24: Ashf 3H 35
Station App. CT15: Mart M 5A 12
TN23: Ashf 5D 4 (4G 35)
Station Dr. CT14: Walm 4E 11
Station Rd. CT14: Walm 4E 11
CT15: St Marg, Mart M 6A 12
CT18: Lym'ge 5E 21
CT19: F'stone 1F 59
CT21: Hythe 6E 57
TN23: Ashf 5C 4 (4G 35)
TN25: Sme 6A 42
TN26: Hoth 1D 30
TN30: Tent 6A 64
Station Rd. Cl. CT14: Walm 4F 11
Steddy Cl. TN23: Ashf 1D 38
Steeds Cl. TN26: Kgnt 5E 39
Steeds La. TN26: Kgnt 6E 39
Stembrook CT16: Dover 4E 7 (3D 28)
Stembrook Ct. CT16: Dover 5E 7 (3E 29)
Stempe Cl. CT18: H'nge 2H 49
Stephen Ct. CT20: F'stone 3G 5
Stiles Cl. CT19: F'stone 6G 49
Stirling Rd. TN24: Ashf 6H 35
Stockdale Gdns. CT14: Deal 1G 11
Stockham Ct. CT19: F'stone 6E 49
Stock La. TN25: Sme 4A 42
Stoddart Rd. CT19: F'stone 1E 59
Stombers La. CT18: Drel, H'nge 5A 24
Stonebridge Cotts.
TN23: Ashf 6B 4 (5F 35)
Stonegate TN25: Wye 1G 33
STONEHALL 1B 14
Stonehall Rd. CT15: Lyd'n 1B 14
STONE HILL 5G 43
Stone Hill TN25: S'ndge 5G 43
Stone St. CT21: Lymp 4E 55
CT21: N'grn, Wnhgr 2F 55
TN25: Stanf 5F 45
Stoney Path CT14: Walm 1H 11
(off Trafalgar Dr.)
Stonyway La. CT15: Chu H, Hou 6E 27
Stonyway La. CT15: Chu H, Hou 6E 27
STOP 24 SERVICE AREA 6G 45
Storey Cres. CT18: H'nge 5E 25
Stour Centre, The 5D 4 (4G 35)
Stour Cl. TN23: Ashf 4C 34
Stourfields TN24: Kenn 1H 35
Stowell Cl. TN23: Ashf 5A 34
Strand, The CT14: Walm 6H 9
Street, The CT14: Fin 3A 8
CT14: Shol 6D 8
CT15: Gus 3E 17
CT15: Mart 4A 12
CT15: W Hou 6B 26
CT18: H'nge 6H 23
CT18: N'tn 6A 48
CT21: Lymp 5D 54
CT21: Post 3A 46
TN23: Gt Cha 5A 34
TN24: Kenn 4A 32
TN24: W'boro 5D 36
TN25: Mers 3G 41

Street, The TN26: Hoth 2C 30
  TN26: Shad 6C 38
Strond St. CT17: Dover 5D 28
Stroudley Cl. TN24: W'boro 5A 36
Strouts Rd. TN23: Ashf 6B 34
Stuart Ct. CT17: Dover 4C 6
Stuart Ho. CT14: Deal 6F 9
Stuart Rd. CT19: F'stone 1C 60
STUBB'S CROSS 4B 38
Stub Stairs CT15: Chu H 6E 27
Studfall Cl. CT21: Hythe 1H 63
Studio Cl. TN24: Kenn 5H 31
Stumble La. TN23: Kgnt 6F 39
Sturdy Cl. CT21: Hythe 5F 57
Sturges Rd. TN24: Ashf 2B 4 (2F 35)
Suffolk Dr. TN23: Ashf 3E 35
Suffolk Gdns. CT17: Dover 4H 27
Sugarloaf Wlk. CT19: F'stone 5B 50
Summer Cl. CT21: Hythe 5B 56
  TN30: Tent 4C 64
Summer Cl. CT21: Hythe 5E 57
            (off Whitegate Cl.)
Summerhill TN23: Ashf 1C 38
Summerhill Pk. TN24: W'boro 6E 37
Summer Leeze TN24: W'boro 5A 36
Summer Leeze Gdns. TN24: W'boro ..5A 36
Sump Cotts. TN23: Kgnt 6F 39
Sun La. CT21: Hythe 5E 57
Sunningdale Av. CT19: F'stone 6G 49
Sunny Bank CT21: Hythe 5B 56
Sunnyside Cl. CT14: Ripp 4B 10
Sunnyside Cotts. CT14: Deal 5G 9
Sunnyside Pl. CT20: F'stone 3H 5
Sunnyside Rd. CT20: S'gte 4D 58
Sunnyside Vs. CT20: F'stone 3H 5
  TN23: Gt Cha 4A 34
Sun Ri. TN25: Ashf 6D 30
Surrenden Rd. CT19: F'stone 1F 59
Surtees Cl. TN24: W'boro 1A 40
Sussex Av. TN24: Ashf 2A 4 (2F 35)
Sussex Rd. CT19: F'stone 2F 5 (1B 60)
Sutherland Cl. CT21: Hythe 5C 56
Sutherland Rd. CT14: Deal 5G 9
Sutton Cl. CT19: F'stone 6G 49
Sutton La. CT14: R'wld, Ripp 1D 12
Swaffer Way TN23: Ashf 6A 34
Swain Rd. TN30: St Mic, Tent 2B 64
Swallowfield TN24: W'boro 6A 36
Swan Grn. TN25: S'ndge 4B 44
Swan La. TN25: S'ndge 4B 44
Swann Way CT18: H'nge 1G 49
Swanton La. CT15: Lyd'n 2A 14
Swanton Mill 5D 40
Sweet Bay Cres. TN23: Ashf 2B 34
SWINGATE 1H 7 (2F 29)
Swinge Hill CT18: Cap F 1E 51
Swiss Way CT19: F'stone 6E 51
Sycamore Cl. CT21: Hythe 6A 56
Sycamore Dr. CT14: Deal 1F 11
Sycamore La. TN23: Ashf 1C 34
Sydcot Dr. CT14: Deal 3H 9
Sydenham Rd. CT14: Deal 4H 9
Sydney Rd. CT14: Walm 4E 11
Sydney St. TN23: Ashf 5F 35

T

Tabret Cl. TN24: Kenn 5H 31
Tadworth Rd. TN24: Kenn 6H 31
Tallis Ct. CT17: Dover 4A 6
Tally Ho Rd. TN26: Shad, Stu X ...5D 38
Tangier Cl. CT15: Gus 6E 17
Tanners Cl. CT21: Hythe 3D 56
Tanner's Hill CT21: Hythe 3E 57
Tanner's Hill Gdns.
  CT21: Hythe 3E 57
Tannery La. TN23: Ashf 4C 4 (3G 35)
Target Firs CT16: Temp E 4F 15
Tar Path CT14: Deal 5G 9
Taswell Cl. CT16: Dover 3F 7 (3E 29)
Taswell St. CT16: Dover 3F 7 (3E 29)
Taylor Rd. CT19: F'stone 1E 59
Taylors Yd. TN25: Wye 1G 33
Taymouth Ho. CT16: Dover 3F 7
Taywood Cl. TN24: W'boro 4B 36
Teal Cl. CT18: H'nge 2F 49
TEDDARS LEAS 1H 47

Teddars Leas Rd. CT18: Etch'l 2F 47
Telegraph Rd. CT14: Deal 3F 11
Telford Ct. CT19: F'stone 1H 5 (1C 60)
Temeraire Hgts. CT20: S'gte 4C 58
Templar Rd. CT16: Temp E 4F 15
Templar St. CT17: Dover 3B 6 (3C 28)
Temple Cl. CT16: Temp E 3F 15
  TN23: Kgnt 2D 38
TEMPLE EWELL 4F 15
Templer Way TN23: Ashf 2E 35
Templeside CT16: Temp E 4F 15
Tennyson Pl. CT19: F'stone 6C 50
Tennyson Rd. TN23: Ashf 1E 39
TENTERDEN 6A 64
Tenterden Golf Course 5D 64
Tenterden Leisure Cen. 6B 64
Tenterden Mus. 6A 64
Tenterden Town Station
    Kent & East Sussex Railway 5A 64
Terlingham La. CT18: H'nge 3G 49
Terminus Wlk. CT20: F'stone 1C 60
            (off The Tram Rd.)
Thanet Gdns. CT19: F'stone 1D 60
Thanet Ter. TN26: Hoth 2C 30
The . . . . . .
  Names prefixed with 'The' for example
  'The Abbots' are indexed under the main
  name such as 'Abbots, The'.
Theatre Sq. TN30: Tent 6A 64
Theatre St. CT21: Hythe 5E 57
Theresa Rd. CT21: Hythe 6D 56
Thirlmere Rd. TN24: Kenn 5H 31
Thistledown CT14: Walm 5F 11
Thomas Cl. TN23: Ashf 1E 39
Thompson Cl. CT14: Walm 5F 11
  CT19: F'stone 6H 49
Thompson Rd. TN24: Ashf 6F 31
Thornbridge Rd. CT14: Deal 2E 11
Thorndike Rd. TN29: Burm 5A 62
Thornlea TN23: Ashf 3C 34
Thornton Cl. TN24: W'boro 4C 36
Thornton's La. CT16: Dover 5F 7
            (off Mill La.)
Three Acres Site CT19: F'stone 6A 50
Three Flds. Path TN30: Tent 6A 64
Three Posts La. CT21: Hythe 5E 57
Throwley Ct. TN23: Ashf 1E 39
            (off Matfield Cl.)
Tiber Cl. CT19: F'stone 1C 58
Tides Leisure Cen. 6G 9
Tilden Gill Rd. TN30: Tent 6C 64
Tile House, The CT21: Hythe 5E 57
            (off Mount St.)
Tile Kiln La. CT19: F'stone 6F 49
Tile Kiln Rd. TN24: Kenn 4G 31
Tilers Wlk. TN24: Kenn 4G 31
Timeball Tower Mus. 5H 9
Timperley Cl. CT14: Deal 5E 9
Tintagel Ho. CT20: F'stone 4H 5
Tithe Barn La. TN23: Ashf 5B 34
Toke Cl. TN23: Gt Cha 4A 34
Toll Ga. CT14: Deal 1E 11
Tolputt Cl. CT19: F'stone 2H 5 (1C 60)
Tolsford Cl. CT18: Etch'l 2F 47
  CT19: F'stone 1D 58
Tontine St. CT20: F'stone 3G 5 (2B 60)
Tormore M. CT14: Deal 1E 11
Tormore Pk. CT14: Deal 1E 11
Toronto Cl. CT16: Dover 6B 16
Torrington Rd. TN23: Ashf 5F 35
Tourist Info. Cen.
    Ashford 4C 4 (3F 35)
    Deal 5H 9
    Dover 4D 6 (3D 28)
    Tenterden 6A 64
Tournay Cl. TN23: Ashf 5D 34
Tourney Cl. CT21: Lymp 4D 54
Tower Cl. CT17: Dover 3C 6 (3C 28)
  CT20: S'gte 4E 59
Tower Gdns. CT21: Hythe 6E 57
TOWER HAMLETS 3A 6 (3C 28)
Tower Hamlets Rd. CT17: Dover ..3B 6 (3C 28)
Tower Hamlets St. CT17: Dover ..3B 6 (3C 28)
Tower Hill CT17: Dover 4B 6 (3C 28)
Tower Point TN23: Ashf 3A 4
Tower St. CT17: Dover 4B 6 (3C 28)
Towers Vw. TN24: Kenn 4G 31
Tower Theatre, The 3D 58
Townsend Farm Rd. CT15: St Marg 3D 18

Townsend Ter. CT17: Dover 6B 28
Town Wlk. CT20: F'stone 5F 5 (3B 60)
Townwall St. CT16: Dover 5F 7 (4E 29)
Trafalgar Dr. CT14: Walm 1H 11
Trafalgar Rd. CT15: St Marg 6D 12
Tram Road, The CT20: F'stone ...4H 5 (2C 60)
Travers Rd. CT14: Deal 6E 9
Trefoil Cl. CT16: Dover 1B 28
Trefor Jones Ct. CT17: Dover 5B 36
Trenchard Cl. TN24: W'boro 5B 36
Trimworth Rd. CT19: F'stone 1F 59
Trinity Ct. CT14: Deal 1E 11
Trinity Cres. CT20: F'stone 3H 59
Trinity Gdns. CT20: F'stone 3A 60
Trinity Homes CT14: Walm 4G 11
Trinity Pl. CT14: Deal 1E 11
Trinity Rd. CT20: F'stone 3H 59
  TN25: Ashf, Kenn 6F 31
Tristram Way CT16: Whitf 4A 16
Tritton Cl. TN24: Kenn 4B 32
Tritton Flds. TN24: Kenn 4A 32
Troubridge Cl. TN24: W'boro 6C 36
Trumpet Ho. TN23: Ashf 5F 35
Trunley Way CT18: H'nge 2F 49
Tudor Byway TN24: Kenn 5H 31
Tudor End TN24: Kenn 6H 31
Tudor Farm Cl. TN23: Kgnt 4E 39
Tudor Ho. CT14: Deal 6E 9
Tudor M. CT14: Deal 1F 11
Tudor Rd. CT19: F'stone 1D 58
  TN24: Kenn 6H 31
  TN26: Hoth 1D 30
Tufton Rd. TN24: Ashf 3H 35
Tufton St. TN23: Ashf 4B 4 (3F 35)
Tufton Wlk. TN23: Ashf 4B 4 (3F 35)
Tumbledown Hill TN25: Westw 1E 31
Tunbridge Way TN23: Ashf 5A 34
Turketel Rd. CT20: F'stone 2G 59
Turner Cl. TN24: Ashf 6A 36
Turner Ct. CT20: F'stone 2F 59
Turners Av. TN30: Tent 5A 64
Turnpike Cl. CT21: Hythe 5C 56
Turnpike Hill CT21: Hythe 4C 56
Tutsham Ct. TN24: Kenn 6G 31
Tweed Ter. CT21: Hythe 5C 56
Twelve Acres TN24: W'boro 5A 36
Twiss Av. CT21: Hythe 5F 57
Twiss Gro. CT21: Hythe 5F 57
Twiss Rd. CT21: Hythe 5F 57
Tye La. CT18: H'nge 6G 23
Tyson Rd. CT19: F'stone 6C 50

U

Uden Rd. TN29: Dym 5F 63
Ulley Rd. TN24: Kenn 4H 31
Undercliff CT20: S'gte 4E 59
Undercliffe Rd. CT14: Kgdn 2H 13
Underdown Rd. CT17: Dover 6A 6 (4B 28)
Underhill Cotts. CT18: Peene 5B 48
Underhill Rd. CT20: F'stone 1B 58
Underwood CT18: H'nge 5A 24
Underwood Cl. TN24: Kenn 5H 31
Underwood Gdns. CT20: S'gte 4F 59
Union Rd. CT14: Deal 5G 9
Union St. CT17: Dover 5D 28
University Centre Folkestone 4G 5
Updike Pl. CT17: Dover 4A 6 (3B 28)
Uphill CT18: H'nge 1H 49
Up. Bridge St. TN25: Wye 1G 33
Upper Corniche CT20: S'gte 4C 58
UPPER DEAL 1D 10
Up. Denmark Rd. TN23: Ashf 5F 35
Up. Malthouse Hill CT21: Hythe 5D 56
Upper Pemberton TN25: Ashf 4F 31
Up. Queens Rd. TN24: Ashf 1B 4 (2F 35)
Upper Rd. CT15: Dover, St Marg 6A 18
  CT16: Dover 2G 7 (2E 29)
Upper St. CT14: Kgdn 2G 13
Up. Vicarage Rd. TN24: Kenn 4H 31
UPPER WALMER 4E 11
Upton Cl. CT19: F'stone 6G 49

V

Valebrook Cl. CT20: F'stone 2C 58
Vale Rd. CT14: Ripp, Sutt 5A 10
  CT15: Sutt 5A 10

Valestone Cl. CT21: Hythe 3B 58
Vale Vw. Rd. CT17: Dover 5A 6 (4B 28)
Valley Cotts. CT15: Alk 2G 25
Valley Rd. CT4: Elham 1H 21
  CT17: Dover 6G 15
  CT20: S'gte 3E 59
Valley Wlk. CT21: Hythe 4A 58
Vancouver Rd. CT16: Dover 6C 16
Varne Pl. CT19: F'stone 1D 60
Varne Ridge Holiday Pk. CT18: Cap F ...3H 51
Varne Rd. CT19: F'stone 2D 60
Vernon Pl. CT14: Deal 3H 9
Vespasian Way TN23: Kgnt 3D 38
Viaduct, The CT17: Dover 6D 28
Viburnum Cl. TN23: Ashf 3C 34
Vicarage, The CT15: St Marg 3D 18
                    (off St Georges Pl.)
Vicarage La. CT4: Elham 2H 21
  CT14: Shol 6D 8
  CT15: St Marg 3D 18
  TN23: Ashf 4C 4 (3G 35)
Vicarage Rd. CT20: S'gte 4F 59
Vickers Cl. CT18: H'nge 1G 49
Victoria Av. CT15: St Marg 3D 19
  CT21: Hythe 5D 56
Victoria Ct. CT21: Hythe 6E 57
                     (off Victoria Rd.)
Victoria Cres. CT16: Dover 3D 6 (3C 28)
  TN23: Ashf 5B 4 (4F 35)
Victoria Gro. CT20: F'stone 4F 5 (2B 60)
  CT21: Hythe 5B 58
VICTORIA HOSPITAL 6F 9
Victoria M. CT14: Deal 5G 9
  CT17: Dover 1A 6
  CT20: F'stone 5E 5
Victoriana Mus. 5H 9
               (within Town Hall, High St.)
Victoria Pde. CT14: Deal 6H 9
Victoria Pk. CT16: Dover 3F 7 (3E 29)
Victoria Pk. M. CT16: Dover 4G 7
Victoria Pl. CT21: Salt 3D 56
Victoria Rd. CT14: Deal 6H 9
  CT14: Kgdn 4F 13
  CT18: Cap F 3F 51
  CT19: F'stone 3E 5 (2A 60)
  CT21: Hythe 5D 56
  TN23: Ashf 5B 4 (4F 35)
Victoria St. CT17: Dover 1A 6 (2B 28)
Victoria Ter. CT21: Hythe 5D 56
Victoria Way TN23: Ashf 5A 4 (4E 35)
Victory Rd. CT15: St Marg 1C 18
Villiers Ct. CT17: Dover 6B 6 (4C 28)
Vincent Cl. CT20: F'stone 3E 59
Vincent Pl. TN24: Kenn 1B 36
Vincers Cotts. TN25: Sme 2E 43
Vineys Gdns. TN30: Tent 4C 64
Violet Way TN23: Kgnt 5G 39
Vlissingen Dr. CT14: Deal 3G 9

W

Waddington Dr. CT18: H'nge 1G 49
Wainwright Pl. TN24: Ashf 5H 35
Wakefield Wlk. CT21: Hythe 6E 57
Wakefield Way CT21: Hythe 6D 56
Walcheren Cl. CT14: Deal 2G 9
Wallace M. CT19: F'stone 6B 50
Wallis Rd. TN24: Ashf 3H 35
Wall Rd. TN24: Ashf 2B 4 (2F 35)
WALMER 4F 11
Walmer & Kingsdown Golf Course ...3H 13
Walmer Castle & Gardens 4H 11
Walmer Castle Rd. CT14: Walm 4G 11
Walmer Ct. CT14: Walm 4F 11
Walmer Gdns. CT14: Deal 3E 11
Walmer Paddling Pool 1H 11
Walmer Station (Rail) 4E 11
Walmer Way CT14: Deal 3E 11
  CT20: F'stone 2F 59
Walmsley Ho. CT19: F'stone ...1H 5 (1C 60)
Walnut Cl. TN24: Kenn 5H 31
Waltham Cl. TN24: W'boro 3C 36
Waltham Pl. TN23: Ashf 1D 38
Walton Gdns. CT19: F'stone 6B 50
Walton Mnr. Cl. CT19: F'stone 5B 50
Walton Rd. CT19: F'stone 1F 5 (1B 60)
Waltons, The CT19: F'stone 5A 50
Warden Ct. CT17: Dover 2C 6 (2C 28)

Warden Ho. M. CT14: Deal 1E 11
Warehouse, The CT17: Dover 4E 7
                   (off Worthington St.)
WARREN, THE 6E 31
Warren, The CT18: Cap F, F'stone ...6E 51
  CT19: F'stone 6E 51
  TN25: Bra L 2E 43
Warren Cl. CT19: F'stone 1D 60
Warren Hgts. TN25: Bra L 2F 43
Warren La. CT15: Ewe M, Lyd'n 2A 14
  TN24: Ashf 1E 35
Warren Retail Park, The TN24: Ashf ...1F 35
Warren Rd. CT19: F'stone 1D 60
Warren Vw. TN25: Ashf 1D 34
Warren Way CT19: F'stone 1D 60
Warwick Rd. CT14: Walm 3H 11
  TN24: Kenn 5A 32
Washford Farm Rd. TN23: Ashf 2C 38
Washington Cl. CT16: Dover 6B 16
WATERBROOK 2C 40
Waterbrook Av. TN24: Ashf 2B 40
Watercress La. CT14: Deal 2B 40
Waterfall Rd. TN26: Hoth 6A 30
Water Farm CT4: Elham 2H 21
Waterloo Cres. CT16: Dover 6F 7 (5D 28)
  CT17: Dover 6E 7 (5D 28)
Waterloo Mans. CT17: Dover 6F 7 (4D 28)
Waterloo Rd. CT20: F'stone 2D 58
Waterloo Ter. TN25: S'ndge 4A 44
Waterman Ho. TN23: Ashf 6A 4 (5F 35)
Watermead Cl. TN23: Ashf 6D 34
Watersend CT16: Temp E 4E 15
Waterside TN24: W'boro 4B 36
Waterside Ct. CT21: Hythe 5D 56
Water St. CT14: Deal 4H 9
Waterworks La. CT15: Mart 4A 12
Watery La. TN25: Westw 3A 30
Watkin Rd. CT19: F'stone 1E 5 (1A 60)
Watsons Ct. TN25: Ashf 3G 31
Watts Cotts. TN24: Kenn 4H 31
Wayside TN30: St Mic 3B 64
Wayside Av. TN30: St Mic 2B 64
Wayside Flats TN30: St Mic 3B 64
Weald, The TN24: Ashf 1C 4 (2G 35)
Wealden Av. TN30: Tent 3B 64
Wear Bay Cres. CT19: F'stone 1D 60
Wear Bay Rd. CT19: F'stone 6D 50
Weavers Way CT16: Dover 6A 16
  TN23: Ashf 4B 34
Webb Cl. CT19: F'stone 6G 49
Webster Way CT18: H'nge 6H 23
Weighbridge Way TN26: Dover 2H 29
Wellesley Av. CT14: Walm 2G 11
Wellesley Rd. CT16: Dover 5F 7 (4E 29)
  TN24: Ashf 3C 4 (4G 35)
Wellesley Vw. TN24: Ashf 3C 4
Wellesley Vs. CT21: Hythe 5B 58
  TN24: Ashf 2C 4
Wellfield Rd. CT20: F'stone 2G 59
Wellington Ct. CT14: Walm 2H 11
                     (off Dover Rd.)
  CT14: Deal 6G 9
                     (off London Rd.)
Wellington Gdns. CT16: Dover 6B 16
Wellington Pde. CT14: Kgdn, Walm ...5H 11
Wellington Pl. CT20: S'gte 4D 58
Wellington Rd. CT14: Deal 6H 9
  CT16: Temp E 4F 15
  CT20: F'stone 2D 58
Wellington Ter. CT20: S'gte 4D 58
                     (off The Esplanade)
Well La. CT15: St Marg 3D 18
Well Rd. CT18: Lym'ge 5E 21
Wells Cl. TN30: Tent 5A 64
Wells Rd. CT19: F'stone 1F 59
Welson Rd. CT20: F'stone 2F 59
Wentworth Cl. CT18: Lym'ge 5E 21
Wesley School Rd. TN23: Ashf 6B 34
Wesley Ter. CT18: Lym'ge 4E 21
Westbourne TN23: Ashf 1B 38
Westbourne Ct. CT20: F'stone 3F 59
Westbourne Gdns. CT20: F'stone 3H 59
Westbury Cres. CT17: Dover 6A 6 (5B 28)
Westbury Pl. CT17: Dover 6A 6 (5B 28)
Westbury Rd. CT17: Dover 6A 6 (5B 28)
Westchurch Ho. TN23: Ashf 6A 4 (4F 35)
WEST CLIFFE 3B 18
W. Cliff Gdns. CT20: F'stone ...5G 5 (3B 60)
Westcliff Ho. CT20: F'stone 5G 5

West Cross TN30: Tent 6A 64
W. Cross Gdns. TN30: Tent 6A 64
W. Cross M. TN30: Tent 6A 64
Westdean Cl. CT17: Dover 1G 27
WESTENHANGER 1F 55
Westenhanger Station (Rail) 6F 45
Westerhout Cl. CT14: Deal 4G 9
Western Av. TN23: Ashf 2A 4 (3E 35)
Western Cl. CT17: Dover 5C 28
Western Gdns. TN24: W'boro 5D 36
Western Ho. CT14: Deal 4G 9
Western Rd. CT14: Deal 5G 9
Western Service Rd. CT16: Dover ...3G 29
Western Vs. TN24: Kenn 5H 31
Westfield Dr. CT16: Whitf 1A 16
Westfield La. CT18: Etch'l 3E 47
WEST HOUGHAM 6B 26
WEST HYTHE 6F 55
W. Hythe Rd. CT21: W Hyt 1E 63
Westland Way CT18: H'nge 2H 49
W. Lawn Gdns. CT20: S'gte 4D 58
West Lea CT14: Deal 4G 9
West Lea Ct. CT14: Deal 4G 9
Westlea Ct. CT20: F'stone 4G 59
Westmoors TN23: Ashf 1C 38
W. Norman Rd. CT16: Dover 2G 7 (3E 29)
West Pde. CT21: Hythe 6D 56
West Ramp CT16: Dover 3G 29
West Rd. CT20: F'stone 3C 58
West St. CT14: Deal 4H 9
  CT17: Dover 3B 6 (3C 28)
  TN23: Ashf 3A 4 (3F 35)
  TN26: Hoth 1C 30
West Ter. CT20: F'stone 5F 5 (3B 60)
West Vw. CT19: F'stone 5B 50
Westwell CT20: F'stone 3C 58
Westwell La.
  TN25: Westw, Hoth ...2B 30, 1A 30 & 3C 30
                        (not continuous)
  TN26: Ashf 5C 30
Weymouth Cl. CT19: F'stone 6D 48
Weymouth Rd. CT19: F'stone 1D 58
Weymouth Ter. CT19: F'stone 6D 48
                 (off Biggins Wood Rd.)
Wharton Gdns. TN24: W'boro 5A 36
Wheatsheaf La. CT15: Mart 4A 12
Whewell Ter. CT20: F'stone 3H 5
Whigham Ct. TN23: Ashf 5B 34
Whinless Rd. CT17: Dover 3A 28
Whitby Rd. CT20: F'stone 1D 58
Whitby Ter. CT16: Dover 6B 16
                     (off Green La.)
White Acre Dr. CT14: Walm 5F 11
Whitebeam Cl. TN23: Ashf 1B 34
White Cliffs CT20: F'stone 6F 5 (3B 60)
White Cliffs Bus. Pk. CT16: Whitf ...4A 16
White Cliffs Pk. CT18: Cap F 3H 51
                        (not continuous)
Whitecliff Way CT19: F'stone 1D 60
White Ct. CT20: S'gte 4E 59
Whitegates Cl. CT17: Dover 6E 57
Whitehall Way TN25: S'ndge 4B 44
White Hill CT15: Alk 1G 25
White Horse Hill CT18: H'nge 2A 50
White Horse La. CT4: R Min 1C 20
Whitenbrook CT21: Hythe 4A 58
Whitenbrook Dell CT21: Hythe 4A 58
White Willow Cl. TN24: W'boro 1H 39
Whitfield Cotts. TN23: Ashf 5F 35
Whitfield Rd. TN23: Ashf 5F 35
Whitfield Vs. TN23: Ashf 5F 35
WHITFIELD 3A 16
Whitfield Av. TN23: Ashf 1B 28
Whitfield Ct. CT16: Whitf 3A 16
Whitfield Hill CT16: Whitf 5G 15
                        (not continuous)
Whitfield Ho. TN23: Ashf 1C 38
Whitfield Rdbt. CT16: Whitf 3A 16
Whitworth Ct. CT18: H'nge 2F 49
Whyte Cl. CT16: Whitf 4B 16
Wickenden Cres. TN24: W'boro 5C 36
Wicker Wlk. CT18: H'nge 2F 49
                     (off Lewis Rd.)
Wickets, The TN24: W'boro 6B 36
Widgeon Wlk. CT18: H'nge 2H 49
Widred Rd. CT17: Dover 3B 6 (3C 28)
Wilberforce Rd. CT20: S'gte 4E 59

Wilkinson Dr. CT14: Walm 2H 11
WILLESBOROUGH 5B 36
Willesborough Ct. TN24: W'boro 3C 36
Willesborough Ind. Pk. TN24: W'boro 4C 36
WILLESBOROUGH LEES 4C 36
Willesborough Rd. TN24: Kenn, W'boro . .6B 32
Willesborough Windmill 4C 36
William Av. CT19: F'stone 6H 49
WILLIAM HARVEY HOSPITAL 4E 37
William Judge Cl. TN30: Tent 6D 64
William Lambert Pl. TN23: Ashf 2C 34
William Muge Ho. CT16: Dover 2E 7
William Pitt Av. CT14: Deal 5F 9
William Pitt Cl. CT21: Hythe 5F 57
William Rd. TN23: Ashf 5F 35
William Stuart Dr. TN23: Ashf 2C 34
Willingdon TN23: Ashf 2C 38
Willingdon Pl. CT14: Walm 4G 11
Willingdon Rd. CT16: Whitf 4A 16
Willop Cl. TN29: Dym 6D 62
Willop Way TN29: Dym 6D 62
Willow Bank TN24: W'boro 3C 36
Willow Cl. CT21: Hythe 6A 56
Willow Cl. CT20: S'gte 3E 59
Willow Ho. TN23: Ashf 4D 34
Willow Rd. CT14: Gt Mon 2A 10
Willows, The TN24: Kenn 5H 31
Willow Tree TN30: Tent 6A 64
(off Highbury La.)
Willow Tree Cl. TN24: W'boro 4B 36
Willow Tree Farm CT21: Hythe 1H 63
Willow Woods Rd. CT14: L Mon 2A 10
Wilson Av. CT14: Deal 2D 10
Wilson Cl. TN24: W'boro 4C 36
Wiltie Ct. CT19: F'stone 3E 5 (2A 60)
Wiltie Gdns. CT19: F'stone 3E 5 (2A 60)
Wilton Cl. CT14: Deal 6F 9
Wilton Rd. CT19: F'stone 1H 59
Winant Way CT16: Dover 6B 16
Winchelsea Ct. CT17: Dover 5B 6 (4B 28)
Winchelsea Rd. CT17: Dover 5A 6 (4B 28)
Winchelsea St. CT17: Dover 5A 6 (4B 28)
Winchelsea Ter. CT17: Dover 5A 6 (4B 28)
Winchester M. CT14: Deal 2F 11
Windermere Ct. TN24: Ashf 1G 35
Windmill Cl. TN24: W'boro 4C 36
Windmill St. CT21: Hythe 6D 56
Windsor Ct. CT14: Walm 3G 11
TN23: Ashf 6B 34
Windsor Ho. CT14: Deal 6E 9
CT17: Dover 5D 6
Winehouse La. CT18: Cap F 2G 51

Wine Pine Ho. CT21: Hythe 6C 56
Wingate Rd. CT19: F'stone 6B 50
Wingleton La. CT14: Ripp, Sutt 6A 10
CT15: Sutt 6A 10
Wingrove Hill CT17: Dover 1G 27
Winkland Oaks Rd. CT14: Ripp 3A 12
CT15: Sutt 3A 12
Winnipeg Cl. CT16: Dover 6C 16
Winslade Ter. TN24: W'boro 4C 36
(off Silver Hill Rd.)
Winslade Way TN24: W'boro 4C 36
Winston Ho. CT20: F'stone 2F 59
Winterage La. CT18: Acr 4B 22
Winter Dr. CT18: H'nge 6H 23
WITHERSDANE 3H 33
Withersdane Cotts. TN25: Wye 1H 33
Witley Wlk. CT16: Whitf 2B 16
Wivenhoe TN23: Ashf 2C 38
Wolfe Ter. CT16: Dover 6B 16
(off Montreal Cl.)
Wollaston Rd. CT14: Walm 1H 11
Wolseley Pl. TN24: Ashf 2B 4 (2F 35)
WOLVERTON .1A 26
Wolverton Hill CT15: Alk 6A 14
Women's Land Army Museum, The 6G 27
Wood Av. CT19: F'stone 6B 50
Woodbury Gdns. TN30: Tent 6A 64
Woodbury La. TN30: Tent 6A 64
Woodchurch Rd. TN26: Shad 5C 38
TN30: Tent 5C 64
Woodcock Gdns. CT18: H'nge 1F 49
Wood Cott. La. CT19: F'stone 6D 48
Woodfield Av. CT19: F'stone 6E 49
Woodfield Cl. CT19: F'stone 6D 48
WOODLAND 4B 20
Woodland Cl. CT17: Dover 1G 27
Woodland Cotts. CT18: Lym'ge 4D 20
Woodland Dr. CT18: H'nge 6H 23
Woodland Ri. CT21: W Hyt 6E 55
Woodland Rd. CT18: Lym'ge 3A 20
Woodlands Dr. CT21: Hythe 3A 58
Woodlands Rd. TN24: W'boro 3B 35
Woodland Way TN29: Dym 4E 63
Wood La. TN23: Kgnt 4G 39
Woodlea TN24: Ashf 1D 4 (2G 35)
Woodlees Cl. TN25: S'ndge 4A 44
Wood Rd. CT21: Hythe 6E 57
Woodside TN23: Ashf 1C 38
Woodside Cl. CT16: Dover 5G 15
Woodside Vw. CT16: Dover 4G 15
Wood's Pl. CT17: Dover 1B 28
Woodstock Rd. CT14: Deal 1G 11

Woodstock Way TN24: Kenn 5G 31
Wood St. CT16: Dover 3D 6 (3C 28)
Wood Yd. CT14: Deal 5H 9
Woolcomber St. CT16: Dover 4F 7 (3E 29)
Woolies, The CT18: Lym'ge 4E 21
Woolmer Dr. TN24: W'boro 6C 36
Woolpack Hill TN25: Sme 2D 42
Woolpack Hill Cotts. TN25: Sme 2D 42
Woolreeds Rd. TN23: Ashf 6E 35
Worthington St. CT17: Dover 4D 6 (3D 28)
Wotton Rd. TN23: Ashf 1E 39
(not continuous)
Wotton Trad. Est. TN23: Ashf 1F 39
Wrights Cl. TN30: Tent 5A 64
Wych Elm Way CT21: Hythe 6A 56
Wycherley Cres. CT16: Dover 5B 16
WYE 1G 33
Wye Bus. Pk. TN25: Wye 1G 33
Wye Fld. Cotts. TN25: Wye 1H 33
Wye Rd. TN25: Bou L 1B 32
Wye Station (Rail) 1F 33
Wyndham Rd. CT17: Dover 4A 6 (3B 28)
Wyndham Way TN25: Ashf 1D 34
Wyndy La. TN25: Ashf 1D 34
Wyvern Way TN24: Ashf 2A 36

Y

Yeoman Gdns. TN24: W'boro 4C 36
Yeomans Sq. TN23: Ashf 5B 34
Yew Cl. TN23: Ashf 3C 34
Yew Tree Cl. CT14: Deal 1E 11
TN25: Stanf 4F 45
Yew Tree Cotts. TN30: St Mic 2B 64
(off Grange Rd.)
Yew Tree M. CT14: Deal 2E 11
York & Albany Cl. CT14: Walm 4F 11
York Ho. CT17: Dover 5E 7 (4D 28)
York M. CT19: F'stone 6E 49
York Rd. CT14: Walm 2H 11
TN24: Kenn 6H 31
York St. CT17: Dover 5E 7 (4D 28)
York St. Rdbt. CT17: Dover 6E 7 (4D 28)
Young Cl. CT14: Deal 5F 9
Young's Pl. CT15: W Hou 6B 26

Z

Zarena Ct. CT20: S'gte 4G 59
Zig Zag Path CT20: F'stone 6E 5 (4A 60)

The representation on the maps of a road, track or footpath is no evidence of the existence of a right of way.

The Grid on this map is the National Grid taken from Ordnance Survey® mapping with the permission of the Controller of Her Majesty's Stationery Office.

SAFETY CAMERA INFORMATION

PocketGPSWorld.com's CamerAlert is a self-contained speed and red light camera warning system for SatNavs and Android or Apple iOS smartphones/tablets. Visit www.cameralert.co.uk to download.

Safety camera locations are publicised by the Safer Roads Partnership which operates them in order to encourage drivers to comply with speed limits at these sites. It is the driver's absolute responsibility to be aware of and to adhere to speed limits at all times.

By showing this safety camera information it is the intention of Geographers' A-Z Map Company Ltd., to encourage safe driving and greater awareness of speed limits and vehicle speed. Data accurate at time of printing.